Overcoming Common Problems Series

Coping with Macular Degeneration
Dr Patricia Gilbert

Coping with the Menopause
Janet Horwood

Coping with a Mid-life Crisis
Derek Milne

Coping with Polycystic Ovary Syndrome
Christine Craggs-Hinton

Coping with Postnatal Depression
Sandra L. Wheatley

Coping with SAD
Fiona Marshall and Peter Cheevers

Coping with Snoring and Sleep Apnoea
Jill Eckersley

Coping with a Stressed Nervous System
Dr Kenneth Hambly and Alice Muir

Coping with Strokes
Dr Tom Smith

Coping with Suicide
Maggie Helen

Coping with Thyroid Problems
Dr Joan Gomez

Curing Arthritis – The Drug-Free Way
Margaret Hills

Curing Arthritis Diet Book
Margaret Hills

Curing Arthritis Exercise Book
Margaret Hills and Janet Horwood

Depression
Dr Paul Hauck

Depression at Work
Vicky Maud

Depressive Illness
Dr Tim Cantopher

Eating Disorders and Body Image
Christine Craggs-Hinton

Eating for a Healthy Heart
Robert Povey, Jacqui Morrell and Rachel Povey

Effortless Exercise
Dr Caroline Shreeve

Fertility
Julie Reid

The Fibromyalgia Healing Diet
Christine Craggs-Hinton

Free Your Life from Fear
Jenny Hare

Getting a Good Night's Sleep
Fiona Johnston

Heal the Hurt: How to Forgive and Move On
Dr Ann Macaskill

Heart Attacks – Prevent and Survive
Dr Tom Smith

Help Your Child Get Fit Not Fat
Jan Hurst and Sue Hubberstey

Helping Children Cope with Anxiety
Jill Eckersley

Helping Children Cope with Change and Loss
Rosemary Wells

Helping Children Get the Most from School
Sarah Lawson

How to Be Your Own Best Friend
Dr Paul Hauck

How to Beat Pain
Christine Craggs-Hinton

How to Cope with Bulimia
Dr Joan Gomez

How to Cope with Difficult People
Alan Houel and Christian Godefroy

How to Improve Your Confidence
Dr Kenneth Hambly

How to Keep Your Cholesterol in Check
Dr Robert Povey

How to Stick to a Diet
Deborah Steinberg and Dr Windy Dryden

How to Stop Worrying
Dr Frank Tallis

Hysterectomy
Suzie Hayman

The Irritable Bowel Diet Book
Rosemary Nicol

Is HRT Right for You?
Dr Anne MacGregor

Letting Go of Anxiety and Depression
Dr Windy Dryden

Lifting Depression the Balanced Way
Dr Lindsay Corrie

Living with Alzheimer's Disease
Dr Tom Smith

Living with Asperger Syndrome
Dr Joan Gomez

Living with Asthma
Dr Robert Youngson

Living with Autism
Fiona Marshall

Overcoming Common Problems Series

Living with Crohn's Disease
Dr Joan Gomez

Living with Diabetes
Dr Joan Gomez

Living with Fibromyalgia
Christine Craggs-Hinton

Living with Food Intolerance
Alex Gazzola

Living with Grief
Dr Tony Lake

Living with Heart Disease
Victor Marks, Dr Monica Lewis and
Dr Gerald Lewis

Living with High Blood Pressure
Dr Tom Smith

Living with Hughes Syndrome
Triona Holden

Living with Loss and Grief
Julia Tugendhat

Living with Lupus
Philippa Pigache

Living with Nut Allergies
Karen Evennett

Living with Osteoarthritis
Dr Patricia Gilbert

Living with Osteoporosis
Dr Joan Gomez

Living with Rheumatoid Arthritis
Philippa Pigache

Living with Sjögren's Syndrome
Sue Dyson

Losing a Baby
Sarah Ewing

Losing a Child
Linda Hurcombe

**Make Up or Break Up: Making the Most of
Your Marriage**
Mary Williams

Making Friends with Your Stepchildren
Rosemary Wells

Making Relationships Work
Alison Waines

Overcoming Anger
Dr Windy Dryden

Overcoming Anxiety
Dr Windy Dryden

Overcoming Back Pain
Dr Tom Smith

Overcoming Depression
Dr Windy Dryden and Sarah Opie

Overcoming Impotence
Mary Williams

Overcoming Jealousy
Dr Windy Dryden

**Overcoming Loneliness and Making
Friends**
Márianna Csóti

Overcoming Procrastination
Dr Windy Dryden

Overcoming Shame
Dr Windy Dryden

The PMS Diet Book
Karen Evennett

Rheumatoid Arthritis
Mary-Claire Mason and Dr Elaine Smith

The Self-Esteem Journal
Alison Waines

Shift Your Thinking, Change Your Life
Mo Shapiro

Stress at Work
Mary Hartley

Ten Steps to Positive Living
Dr Windy Dryden

Think Your Way to Happiness
Dr Windy Dryden and Jack Gordon

The Traveller's Good Health Guide
Ted Lankester

**Understanding Obsessions and
Compulsions**
Dr Frank Tallis

When Someone You Love Has Depression
Barbara Baker

Your Man's Health
Fiona Marshall

Overcoming Common Problems

Living with Grief and Loss

Julia Tugendhat

sheldon PRESS

First published in Great Britain in 2005

Sheldon Press
36 Causton Street
London SW1P 4ST

Copyright © Julia Tugendhat 2005

Extract from the New English Bible © Oxford University Press and
Cambridge University Press, 1961, 1970.

British Library Cataloguing-in-Publication Data

A catalogue record for this book is available from the British Library

ISBN 0–85969–944–7

1 3 5 7 9 10 8 6 4 2

Typeset by Deltatype Limited, Birkenhead, Merseyside
Printed in Great Britain by
Ashford Colour Press

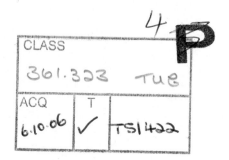

Contents

Introduction   ix

1 Grief   1
2 How grief feels   9
3 How to mourn   19
4 Helping grief along   26
5 Complicated grief   32
6 Losses   40
7 More losses   48
8 Children and grief   57
9 Severe grief   67
10 Ageing and dying   77
   Conclusion   85

   Useful addresses   87
   Further reading   94

This book is dedicated to the memory of Grant Roxburgh

Introduction

My knowledge and understanding of grief come from personal experience and 20 years' work as a systemic psychotherapist with individuals, couples and families. In fact, I deal with grief most days of the week since the majority of people who come to see me professionally are struggling with loss of one kind or another. They might be grieving for a loved one, a significant relationship, a job or a pet. I could go on and on, but the point is that we don't go to therapy to talk about how happy we are. We take this for granted. We might even believe we have a right to happiness. We don't take unhappiness nearly so much for granted although it is also an integral part of everyday life. Grief is the physical, psychological and emotional way we express our pain and sorrow when we lose something to which we are deeply attached. So attachment and love, and loss and sorrow are opposite sides of the same coin.

But it seems that in our society, in this era at least, we are much less prepared for the loss and sorrow side of the coin. We are not accustomed to living with pain, illness, death and disaster as our stoical forebears were. On the contrary, we make great efforts to avoid them, concentrating instead on the pursuit of happiness, material goods and self-fulfilment. We treat loss and sorrow as aberrations and intrusions in our lives. I don't want to go back to the old days, but I believe that we need to know as much about grief as we do about happiness. I hope this book will normalize grief so that readers will be able to understand, accept and manage it when it arises, as it inevitably will. If I have left out grievous situations that are familiar to readers I ask to be forgiven. It is not because I underrate their significance but rather that I am limited for space. I am indebted to friends, colleagues and interviewees who have shared their expertise with me. I am particularly grateful to all my clients over the years who have taught me most of what I know about the human condition.

1
Grief

The terms 'grieving' and 'mourning' are often used interchangeably, but in this book I shall be drawing a distinction between the individual expression of grief and the collective act of mourning, which is the way grief is expressed socially and culturally, for example through rituals like funerals. Grief in relation to loss can be experienced on a continuum of intensity. At the minimal end are the normal losses with which we deal as we pass through transitions in the life cycle. When we are born we are snatched from the cosy warmth of our mothers' wombs into the startling world. As infants we are weaned from the breast. As toddlers we have to learn to leave the security of our primary carers for independent sorties on our own. We leave home to go to school and institutions of further education. In due course we show our independence by setting up our own homes and creating new relationships. Along the way we almost certainly will suffer illnesses, accidents and relationship failures. We will experience the death of grandparents and eventually of parents and friends, until finally we are face to face with our own deaths. The more we are able to deal with these life cycle transitions, the more we gain the strength, resources and confidence to help us withstand the more unexpected challenging losses that might come our way.

These more challenging losses, which are usually intrusions in the life cycle, fall somewhere in the middle of the grief continuum. As a practising psychotherapist I have worked with people who have struggled to adjust to the loss of their homelands through enforced emigration; the loss of a united family through divorce; the loss of mental or physical health; the loss of work; the loss of fertility; and the loss of dreams and ideals. Without attributing any identifiable details, I describe what has happened to them and what has helped them to deal with their grief.

At the intense end of the continuum comes bereavement, which is the death of someone significant. The death of someone we love is traumatic, but some deaths are more traumatic than others. For example, sudden or accidental death, suicide, homicide and the death

1

of a child will have a greater impact than the expected death of a grandparent at the end of a fulfilling life. In later chapters I explain some of these complicated deaths in greater detail, showing what resources can be summoned to help people cope with them.

Our capacity for dealing with separation and loss partly depends on the quality of our earliest attachments to parents (or carers). If these attachments have been solid and secure, we tend to cope well with all the normal separations, like going to school, that we experience as children. When we are adult, our benign childhood experiences will help us to tolerate and recover from deaths or other severe losses that come our way. If, however, our early attachments have been insecure, fraught with anxiety or too frequent, as adults our attachments may be negative and we are more likely to find it difficult to tolerate and recover from separation and loss. I shall go into all this in more detail later on when I explain attachment-and-loss theory that informs our present understanding of grief.

Grief following the death of a loved one is universal to humankind, though it may be expressed in a variety of ways in different cultures. Because grief is such a fundamental and intrinsic part of the human condition it has found expression from time immemorial in song, poetry, literature, music, dance and art throughout the world. In this chapter I turn to more eloquent voices than mine from past history and literature to illustrate in a general way the grief of a parent for a child, of a husband for a wife, of a friend for a friend, and of a brother for a brother. These stories teach us that grief crosses time, cultures, gender, age and class.

Anyone who has lost a child will connect instantly with King David's ancient lament at the death of his son Absalom which is described so vividly in the Old Testament. King David had many sons but his favourite was Absalom. 'In all Israel no man was so much admired for his beauty as Absalom; from the crown of his head to the sole of his foot he was without flaw.' He was also disloyal, ambitious and ultimately treacherous. David tried to be stern but, to the despair of his advisors, always ended up forgiving him. Even when Absalom raised an army against him, David called his own commanders to him before they went into battle and begged them to 'deal gently with the young man Absalom for my sake'.

When Absalom became impaled on the boughs of a tree and was dispatched by some of David's soldiers there was a great reluctance

2

to take this news to the king. Eventually, someone summoned up the courage to tell him.

> The king was deeply moved and went up to the roof-chamber over the gate and wept, crying out as he went, 'O, my son! Absalom my son, my son Absalom! Would that I had died instead of you! O Absalom, my son, my son.' Joab was told that the king was weeping and mourning for Absalom; and that day's victory was turned for the whole army into mourning, and because the troops heard how the king grieved for his son; they stole into the city like men ashamed to show their faces after fleeing from a battle.
>
> 2 Sam. 18.3–19.3

In his great epic poem *The Iliad*, Homer tells of the suffering of the Greek hero Achilles for his dear friend and comrade Patroclus. The grief of Achilles was intensified because of the guilt he felt, having allowed Patroclus to go into battle against the Trojans disguised in his own bronze armour, helmet and shield. Patroclus fought most valiantly but was finally brought down and killed by Hector before being stripped of his armour. For hours the battle raged around his naked body, the Trojans trying to drag it off to dishonour it, the Greeks determined to prevent them. At last they managed to carry his body to safety. When Achilles was told of the death of his friend a black cloud of grief engulfed him.

> He picked up the sooty dust in both his hands and poured it over his head. He begrimed his handsome features with it, and black ashes settled on his sweet-smelling tunic. Great Achilles lay spread out in the dust, a giant of a man, clawing at his hair with his hands and mangling it.
>
> Homer, *The Iliad*

When they had cleaned the body and wrapped it in linen, the Greeks led by Achilles lamented and mourned for Patroclus for the whole night. Achilles vowed to postpone the funeral until he had brought back the head of Hector and the armour he had lost.

One of the great monuments to grief is the Taj Mahal in Agra, India. This jewel of a mosque was built as a mausoleum for his wife by the Moghul Emperor Shah Jahan. Although the Shah could have had many consorts, his young bride Mumtaz Mahal was the only woman he wanted. He admired her for her intelligence and moral virtues as well as her great beauty. She was a devout Muslim who helped the poor and needy. When she died in 1631 giving birth to their fourteenth child he was distraught with grief and immediately started to build a mausoleum for her. No expense was spared and thousands of skilled workers were employed in the construction of this intricately decorated white marble domed building, with its four slender minarets set off by a Moghul water garden. The Taj Mahal has emotional as well as architectural beauty. Tagore, the great Indian poet, described it as 'a tear on the face of eternity'. Unusually for a man in his position at this time, Shah Jahan never took another wife, though he lived for a further 35 years. At the end of his life he was imprisoned, by his son, in a fort from which he could see his wife's mausoleum shimmering in the distance. When he died he was buried beside her.

In the early part of the nineteenth century, before the advent of modern medicine, death could eradicate almost an entire family. The sorrow and pain that the poet John Keats suffered in his short life became a recurring theme and mainspring of his writing. When he was only 15 his mother died. He had already lost his father, a brother and two uncles. He was at boarding school when his mother became ill with tuberculosis. Having nursed her devotedly, he returned to school where his teachers and friends were shocked by the violence of his sorrow. He sometimes became so overwhelmed with emotion that he had to leave his desk and hide in an alcove. But his suffering did not end with his mother's death. Tom, a younger brother whom he loved and cared for, also succumbed to consumption at the age of 19. In the poem he wrote shortly afterwards, Keats questions the purpose of grief.

> I had a dove and the sweet dove died;
> And I have thought it died of grieving.
> O, what could it grieve for? Its feet were tied,
> With a silken thread of my own hands' weaving.
> Sweet little red feet! Why should you die –
> Why should you leave me, sweet bird! Why?
>
> John Keats, 'The Dove'

In 1932, the artist Dora Carrington, known to her Bloomsbury group friends simply as Carrington, chose to end her own life rather than live without Lytton Strachey, whom she adored. Although their relationship was not physical, because Strachey was homosexual, and Carrington had lovers, they lived together in Ham Spray House and were extremely close and interdependent. Strachey, who was 14 years older, was probably more of a father figure to her. Two months after Strachey died of cancer, Carrington was found dying of gunshot wounds at Ham Spray. A verdict of accidental death was given at the inquest, but it is clear from the correspondence of friends like Virginia Woolf and Gerald Brenan that they believed she had committed suicide out of grief for Lytton Strachey.

Did these individuals recover from their bereavements? Dora Carrington manifestly did not. With the passage of time and certain mourning rituals, King David and Achilles rejoined the battle. After Tom's death Keats fell deeply in love with Fanny Brawne and produced an outpouring of poetry, but died tragically young four years later. Generally speaking, the majority of us do recover from bereavement. And strange though it may seem, we recover precisely because we grieve. Grieving is nature's way of helping us to heal. From the men, women and children I have worked with, as well as those I interviewed for this book, I have learnt much about the resilience of human beings in the face of death and loss. I do believe in the restorative power of grief, a subject which I will develop later, but acknowledge that there are some individuals who get stuck and can't move on. I shall discuss why this might happen, and to whom, and suggest what can help.

Collective mourning has a healing effect, too. We will see in a later chapter how funerals serve this function for families and friends. A town can mourn, as Liverpool did when the UK businessman Kenneth Bigley was killed in Iraq in 2004. A nation can mourn, as Britain did for Princess Diana, and the United States did after the terrorist attacks of September 11. It would not be too fanciful to suggest that the whole world mourned after the Tsunami deluge at the end of 2004. More recently, the funeral of Pope John Paul II in April 2005 was described by a newspaper commentator as 'the greatest act of mourning ever seen on the planet'.

The public exhibition of grief manifested after the death of Princess Diana in 1997 was extraordinary. Although the media latched on to the phenomenon, it started spontaneously and caught everyone by surprise. As soon as her death was announced the floral tributes kept on coming until there was a sea of bouquets and teddy bears outside Kensington Palace in Hyde Park. Crowds of solemn and silent people came to look at the flowers and read the attached messages. Long queues formed for the signing of books of condolence. Individuals of every creed and colour flocked to the capital to witness the funeral procession. A woman from Lincoln summed it all up for a television interviewer when she said, 'I have come to share in the grief.'

But what was this all about? First, it was a genuine and heartfelt reaction to the tragic death of a young ill-fated fairy-tale princess. It was a demonstration of sympathy and solidarity towards a vulnerable person many felt had been ill treated by members of the royal family, who were blamed and criticized for not showing their feelings in public. It was a tribute to the charitable work she had done to help people less fortunate than herself. It gave us a legitimate opportunity to express our anger and sorrow in the company of thousands of others doing the same thing. We might have been less conscious of how Diana's death made us aware of our own mortality and triggered feelings of loss in our own lives. Somehow the public expression of grief gave us permission to grieve for ourselves.

Since then a sort of formalized ritual has been created for the expression of public grief. We saw this clearly, albeit on a smaller scale, when Kenneth Bigley, an ordinary British businessman, was beheaded by terrorists in Iraq in 2004. Although he had not lived in his native city for over 20 years, Liverpool went into mourning. Streams of visitors walked to the Bigley family terraced house to leave bouquets of flowers. On 9 October a two-minute silence was observed. This was led by the Lord Mayor and religious leaders outside the town hall. Hundreds of people attended the ceremony where the municipal bell was rung 62 times – for every year of his life. Vigils and prayers were held in the city's cathedrals and churches.

The media can be glib and hyperbolic in the way it exploits grief. The bereaved expose themselves to television interviews and we are asked to empathize with them. We read how the hearts of politicians go out to the grief-stricken members of the family. When three young soldiers from the Black Watch regiment were killed in the Iraq War, the exaggerated headline in *The Times* newspaper read, 'Scotland is in Mourning'. Nevertheless, the media is telling us something about a need in our western society. It seems we crave a demonstrative, collective outlet for our emotions, especially in the event of unpredictable and random disasters which involve large numbers of innocent people.

This was graphically illustrated after the destruction of the Twin Towers and deaths of nearly 3,000 in New York in 2001, a national disaster on a different scale than the death of one woman. Not since the assassination of President Kennedy in 1963 had anything so terrible happened to the nation. The scale of the tragedy, the shock and sense of outrage caused people to gather together to express their grief in churches, in the streets, in civic centres and in community halls. Strangers wept and embraced each other. A sense of altruism swept the nation. Blood, time, skills and money were generously donated for those in need. Support systems sprang up on the Internet. A register of survivors was created and the web became alive with the sharing of stories of miracles and tragedies. Information about how to grieve was made available on a number of websites. Survivors did not have to feel alone in their grief. They were enveloped by a tangible sense of mass solidarity, empathy and support. Much the same phenomenon occurred after innocent people were blown up by terrorists in two trains in Madrid. In this case the king and queen of Spain were in the forefront of the demonstrations of grief.

The Tsunami catastrophe that took 150,000 lives in Asia at the end of 2004 was one of the biggest humanitarian disasters in history. The images on our television screens which showed the scale of the tragedy, the force of nature, the randomness of who died and who survived, the mass graves of Muslims, Buddhists, Christians, wealthy tourists, impoverished locals, young and old, made an impact on the whole world. In Britain this was shown by the public observance of a three-minute silence. Religious services were held up and down the land. The outpouring of goodwill was both tangible and heartening. Disaster funds were set up and money from individuals poured in. There was no shortage of volunteers offering assistance. Governments vied with each other in their pledges of assistance. Reactive emotions such as these may be short-lived and shallow, but there is no doubt they give us a sense of corporate solidarity and help us to deal with emotions stirred up by shocking tragedies.

The most remarkable feature of the death of Pope John Paul II was that it was enacted in the public gaze. The crowds gathered in St Peter's Square to receive the Pope's traditional Easter blessing witnessed the sight of a dying man when he came to the window to give a blessing. For the next seven days, news of the Pope's decline, his thoughts, prayers and actions, were relayed to the faithful outside who wept, prayed and comforted each other. By the day of the funeral on 8 April, it was estimated that five million mourners had gathered in St Peter's Square.

Why were millions of ordinary people prepared to queue for hours and sleep rough in order to get a brief glimpse, if they were lucky, of the dead Pope as he lay in state? The intense media exposure had made them aware that they were participating in a unique historical event. They wanted to be part of this event, not at a distance but in person. They want to express their grief with others who felt the same. They wanted to pay homage and to say goodbye to someone they felt they knew as a friend. John Paul II had been more approachable and accessible through his travels and appearances than any pope in history. One woman said that she had come to Rome to learn about 'a good death' so that she would not be afraid when her time came. A young Polish student said, 'I had to come and say goodbye. I wanted to thank him for all he has done for our country and the world.' There is no doubt that this long-drawn-out collective act of mourning, enacted with so much pomp and ceremony, helped ordinary individuals to come to terms with the loss of a charismatic leader.

2

How grief feels

Grief is a complex mixture of the physical, emotional and mental. It is not a single state of mind, but a long process that changes over time. I have selected three people to recount how it feels. One is the writer and academic C. S. Lewis, whose journal, *A Grief Observed*, is considered a classic. The second is a widow whose husband died very unexpectedly. The third is a sculptor who processed her grief through her art. In the light of expert knowledge and theory I then analyse the components of grief more closely.

Clive Staples Lewis was a confirmed bachelor and Professor of Medieval and Renaissance English at Cambridge University when he met and married an American called Joy Davidson. They had a brief but very happy marriage before she got terminal cancer. The following description is taken from the journal in which he recorded his tumultuous feelings.

> No one ever told me that grief felt so like fear. I am not afraid, but the sensation is like being afraid. The same fluttering in the stomach, the same restlessness, the yawning. I keep on swallowing. At other times it feels like being mildly drunk, or concussed. There is a sort of invisible blanket between the world and me.
>
> C. S. Lewis, *A Grief Observed*

In this much quoted sentence C. S. Lewis vividly describes the mixture of physical and emotional shock experienced by bereaved people.

He compares grief to a bomber circling round and dropping its bombs each time the circle brings it overhead. He senses that his bereavement makes him a social embarrassment to others. At first he cannot visit the places where they had been happy. He panics that he can't remember what his wife looked like, though her voice remains vivid. Worst of all, he begins to question his faith in God. How could a good God allow someone to suffer so? He feels forsaken by God who has slammed the door shut just when he most needed him. He wrestles with the meaning of death and the possibility of an

9

afterlife. Can he really believe that she is now happy and at peace? He finds that the times he is not thinking of her are even worse than the times he is.

And then slowly the anguish and intensity of his emotions began to recede until one day he was able to write that something unexpected had happened – his heart was lighter than it had been for weeks. And he made the curious discovery that when his feelings were less intense he remembered her more clearly. His mind turned back to God and he discovered an open door to his faith.

Michaela, the widow whom I interviewed, spoke in somewhat similar terms of what she had been through when her apparently fit husband of 25 years died of a massive heart attack at her feet.

Losing my life's companion was far worse than my divorce or the death of my parents. At first I was numb with shock. I felt outside myself watching me talking and acting but not there. I got panic attacks and couldn't breathe. I couldn't eat or drink because it was difficult keeping anything down. What frightened me the most was being woken up at night by my own scream. I felt ill. I became obsessed with the thought that if I had acted differently I might have saved him. I rang my brother who is a doctor and several doctor friends incessantly to go over and over the sequence of events. I knew how many minutes it took me to get him to the door on our way to the doctor. Eventually, though not completely, they have reassured me that there was nothing I could have done. Two years on, although I feel stronger, I think I feel more depressed because I have to face up now to the realization that I will live the rest of my life without him; without the partner with whom I shared all the small things of life. The things I miss the most are the physical contact and presence and his sense of humour. Grieving is like dancing the tango – two steps forward and one back. But I am trying to draw strength from the happy memories in the past, to try and enjoy the present and hopefully stop fearing the future. It isn't what happens to you that counts, but how you deal with it. It makes you humble to grieve because you realize that you are so insignificant in comparison to the one you loved. One of the things the vicar told me early on was that 'grief is the price of love'. I also see that you don't need just to react to it. You can participate in it.

The sculptor Jean Parker has described grief in a different language – through a remarkable series of sculpted heads entitled *Bald Statements*. Jean has had more than her fair share of grief. Nine years ago one of her sons and his young wife were tragically killed while climbing in the Rocky Mountains. There followed an extremely painful divorce after 30 years of marriage. Then to cap it all she was diagnosed with cancer of the breast and had to undergo a mastectomy and chemotherapy. It was while she was still very ill that she dug deep inside herself and found an authentic way to express her accumulated grief. During a week when she was on a silent retreat she looked in the mirror every day and moulded eight little heads out of clay. Six of them are bald and express with a raw and startling energy what Jean began to realize were stages of her grief. Later she was able to stand back from these very personal statements and transform the clay models into much larger heads carved out of alabaster. These heads have a more abstract and universal quality.

The first head is disguised by a wig and wears a blank expression. The glacial featureless marble head is gripped in an iron vice. Jean believes this head represents her feelings of shock, numbness and denial. The second head, which is bald, represents her pain, protest and disbelief. The surface of the marble is rough and there is a jagged hole right through it. 'This is the primal scream. For me this was the most painful time. I felt I could have been overwhelmed at any moment.' The third head is full of bewilderment. 'Why me?' it asks. 'Why such suffering?' The fourth bald head is angry. Jean feels that she has not entirely succeeded here because anger was so difficult for her to acknowledge. The skin is flayed and lacerated and the back of the head is hollow. 'This is the stage when I was out of my mind and witless.' The fifth head with big soulful eyes is so heavy with sadness it needs a supporting hand. 'This is a place which was hard to leave because others were able to relate to me with kindness and concern.' Then something happens and the figures become lighter in tone and feeling. The sixth head is upright and the gaze is direct, though one eye is shut. At this stage Jean thinks she is just beginning to readjust to her new reality. The next head has a slight Buddha smile and exudes peace. 'The last figure with hair is me, asleep in the sun. I have relaxed and let go at last.'

What do these descriptions tell us about grief? They tell us about

11

the numbness grief brings and how intensely physical it feels. They tell us about its unpredictable nature: Lewis likens it to a long and winding valley, where any bend may reveal a totally new landscape. The confusion and devastation it caused in their lives is clear. Gradually, however, the intensity of their emotions begins to evaporate until they come to terms with what has happened. The religious belief that meant so much to him is restored to Lewis. He believes that he has got over his wife's death in the way a man who has had a leg amputated gets over the operation. He will continue to feel pain in the stump at times and will always be a one-legged man. Michaela knows that she has to live alone now, but gains strength from past happiness. All three participated positively in the grief process. This was probably instinctive. Lewis tried to make sense of his emotions by chronicling them. Jean Parker gave them physical form and shape. Michaela processed them through talking.

How typical are these reactions and how do they fit with our theoretical understanding of the grief process? In fact they fit very neatly. Much of the research and study has focused on bereavement, because the loss of a loved one is considered the most severe a person can suffer. But the same process, though it might be shorter and less intense, can be experienced with other major losses.

In 1915 Freud wrote a paper which began to articulate his ideas about grief which he termed 'mourning'. He understood the power of attachment to a love object – whether this was a person, a country or an ideal. He knew that the loss of this love object led to great suffering, which for some people ended in depressive illness he termed 'melancholia'. His belief at this point was that the function of mourning was to detach from the memory of the loved one. Years later, in the 1950s and 1960s, a British psychiatrist called Dr John Bowlby conducted scientific studies that led to his formulation of attachment-and-loss theory, which underpins our present understanding of grief. Bowlby had been influenced by the famous ethologists Konrad Lorenz and Nicholaas Tinbergen. Lorenz had done research into the behaviour of geese and found that they could remain faithful to a mate throughout life. He also showed how newly hatched baby goslings attached themselves firmly to the mother goose and cheeped with anxiety if separated from her. Intrigued by these studies of animal behaviour, Bowlby did some observation research on toddlers who were separated from their parents in hospital. These were the days when parents were not encouraged to be with their infants in hospital.

From his research he came to the conclusion that an infant will commonly show a predictable sequence of behaviour when parted from the mother or primary carer. At first, with tears and protests the child demands his mother back and will not be comforted. Later he becomes quieter but is clearly preoccupied and in despair. Eventually, he seems to forget his mother, so that when she comes for him the child seems curiously detached. After returning home he may remain aloof for a while but then becomes intensely clinging, and whenever his mother leaves him, even for a moment, expresses anxiety and rage. With these experiments Bowlby showed the strength of the bond between mother (or primary carer) and infant, and the ill effects of being deprived of this bond. In other words, he showed that babies could express grief.

He went on to extrapolate that the breaking of bonds between humans causes strong emotional reactions.

> In terms of subjective experience, the formation of a bond is described as falling in love, maintaining a bond as loving some-one, and losing a partner as grieving over someone. Similarly, threat of loss arouses anxiety and actual loss causes sorrow; whilst both situations are likely to arouse anger.

John Bowlby, *The Making and Breaking of Affectional Bonds*

Colin Murray Parkes is another British psychiatrist who has had an important influence on our knowledge of grief. He formulated his main theories after studying a group of widows during their first year of bereavement. As a result of his interviews, he identified four stages of mourning, very similar to those identified by Bowlby. First there is numbness, when the prime emotions are shock and disbelief. This is the stage when it is difficult to believe what has happened. Second there is yearning, when the bereaved may feel anger and guilt. The bereaved is physically restless and may go over and over the sequence of events in a compulsive action replay. The third stage is disorganization and despair, when they experience anxiety, loneliness, fear and helplessness. The fourth phase, reorganization, happens when acceptance has taken place. Parkes is clear that the components of grief are psychological and physical. The bereaved

13

often experience breathlessness, heavy limbs, dizziness, panic attacks, restlessness, trouble breathing, sleeplessness, changing eating patterns and loss of concentration. They tend to consult doctors more frequently and report more symptoms of ill health.

Further research, largely by American academics, has added some new dimensions to our theories of grief. The view is that Parkes put too much emphasis on feelings of loss and not enough on the practical tasks of readjustment that people need to do for recovery. There is disagreement, too, with the view that for recovery to occur, the bereaved need to detach from the loved one. Freud himself found that his own experience did not conform to his early theory of detachment. He was inconsolable when his daughter Sophie and his young grandson died. He found he could not detach from his memories and feelings. We now believe that the best way to recover is to internalize the memory of the loved one rather than to detach from it.

The American academic William Worden finds the notion of stages of grief too passive. He conceives of grief as an active process in which various mental, psychological, moral and spiritual tasks need to be accomplished. His guidance, which is specific to bereavement, can be applied to loss of any kind. His four suggested tasks are as follows: to accept the reality of the loss; to experience the pain of grief; to adapt to the world in which the deceased is missing; to emotionally relocate the deceased and move on. Worden recognizes that even when a death is expected, the reality can be denied. The purpose of the first task, therefore, is to face up to the fact that the person has died and will not be coming back. Funerals and rituals help this task along. Experiencing the pain, which is the second task, can be done more easily with the help of others. It is a natural instinct to try and avoid the pain. The task of adapting to a world in which the deceased is missing is very individual and often practical. Much depends on the individual's own circumstances and personality. This stage, too, is painful and can take a long time. To emotionally relocate the deceased and move on, it helps to think of death as the ending of a life but not a relationship. The process of internalizing the deceased can be conscious and unconscious, and continues and changes over time. I very much like Worden's notion that we can take some positive control of our own grief process and move it along, and will give many examples of the creative ways people have found to accomplish these tasks.

Psychologists Stroebe and Schut have a model for grief which takes account of possible differences between men and women. They believe that when a loss occurs, the bereaved has to deal with two things at once: loss and recovery. They call these two tasks loss-orientation and restoration-orientation. The first focuses on the past, while the second focuses on the present and future. People need to oscillate between these two states in the grief process. Difficulties tend to arise if one orientation is emphasized at the expense of the other. Men, for instance, might avoid sadness and pain by launching into work or practical tasks. Women might get so wrapped up in sadness that they cannot move on.

Useful though these theories are for professionals, the trouble with them is that they make the grief process sound too structured and tidy when in fact people experience it as just the opposite. The phases get all jumbled up. Individuals have such different personalities, histories, cultures and role models that his or her grief can take different forms in a widely differing time scale. Emotions are all over the place. There are good days and bad. Moods can be up or down. Concentration and memory disintegrate, which can be scary for normally efficient people. When we are grief-stricken we can lose our sense of judgement and do crazy and uncharacteristic things. We can feel alarmingly out of control. When my mother died I had a manic desire to clear out her house and get rid of her possessions, most of which I consigned to a bonfire. I even sold some silver objects that I inherited from her. Maybe my relatives tried to stop me. If so I paid no attention and, of course, much regret not having kept more to remember her by.

Michaela, whom I have quoted above, did experience a grief pattern that approximates to Worden's template. But I have worked with another widow, whose husband committed suicide, who hardly grieved at all. She had lived with her husband's depression and threats to end his life for so many years that she was prepared for his death, felt a sense of relief, and was comforted by a belief that her husband was at peace at last. Nevertheless, I shall analyse some of the feelings involved in grief even though they might not be experienced by everyone and certainly not in any particular sequence.

Numbness is a feeling of disassociation, or being in a state of suspended animation. Michaela described it as if she was a detached person, watching herself talking and acting but not there. Her body, meanwhile, reacted very strongly to the trauma with physical symptoms that persisted for months. She couldn't eat or sleep properly. She had panic attacks and felt breathless. During this numb phase she acted like a robot – going through day-to-day motions without being fully aware of what she was doing. What she may not have realized, though, was how helpful this numbness was, even if it did feel weird. It is in fact a healthy and natural reaction to shock and acts as a defence mechanism, temporarily keeping at bay feelings of pain and sorrow that would initially be too overwhelming. Michaela went through a yearning stage, too, when she obsessively went over the details of what had happened, blaming herself for not having been able to get her husband to hospital in time to save him.

When we are grieving, anger and the more extreme emotion of rage can take us by surprise. We can feel furious with our loved ones for dying or abandoning us and changing our lives forever. These powerful feelings can be directed against all sorts of unsuspecting people as well. Our anger might be directed against medical professionals if things have gone wrong, or even just because they were involved. We are very sensitive when we are grieving and can get upset with friends or relatives who are crass or unhelpful. Wills and legacies can bring out the worst in families and we can feel affronted by greedy, grasping relatives. We might just rail against fate or, like C. S. Lewis, against God. We might resent friends who are happy when we are not.

It is important to remember that anger is a natural and healthy emotion. Being able to acknowledge and express it is energizing and acts as an antidote to depression. Bowlby goes further, claiming that:

> anger is a necessary condition for mourning to run a healthy course. Only after every effort has been made to recover the person lost, it seems, is the individual in a mood to admit defeat and to orient himself afresh to a world from which the loved person is accepted as irretrievably missing.

John Bowlby, *The Making and Breaking of Affectional Bonds*

Guilt can be corrosive and damaging to self-esteem, but in grief we tend to feel it nevertheless. It can be closely enmeshed with anger.

For a start, we can be angry at ourselves for the guilt we feel. We blame ourselves for things we did and things we didn't do. We might feel that we have done something so wrong that we are despicable or horrible. We might displace our feelings of guilt on to others as blame and anger. For instance, if a loved one dies alone in a home or in a hospital, we might feel guilty for not having visited enough, so we might focus our negative feelings on the professional carers.

Guilt is not necessarily bad in itself. It can serve as a moral compass. In his popular book *Further Along the Road Less Travelled*, Scott Peck writes,

> we need a certain amount of guilt in order to exist in society. And that's what I call existential guilt. I hasten to stress, however, that too much guilt, rather than enhancing our existence, impedes it. This is neurotic guilt. It is like walking around a golf course with eighty-seven clubs in your bag instead of fourteen, which is the number needed to play optimal golf.

If we are conscious of what we are feeling guilty about we might be able to make amends, even in an indirect way. We might be able to compensate for it, thereby cancelling it out. Or we might find a way to forgive ourselves. Guilt can stem from a feeling of excessive responsibility that does not always fit the facts or the broader picture. Feelings of regret and guilt get conflated and it is worth trying to disentangle them. We can regret the lack *of* something that should not have the same weight as feeling directly culpable *for* something.

Feelings of confusion and powerlessness can be frightening. The severe shock to the system affects memory and concentration for months. We can find ourselves below par at work, unable to make decisions and unclear about everything. This is all to be expected, and employers and anyone involved should try and be as understanding and patient as possible. We will find our competencies gradually returning with time. What does not return so quickly is our self-esteem. Losing something precious, whether it is a person or a country, a united family, a job or a happy childhood, can knock our self-confidence to smithereens. So much of our identity and personality may be tied up with what has been lost that we feel adrift and de-skilled. This is hardly surprising if the foundations, which have provided our security, have been pulled out from under us. But in time most of us do recover a sense of self, even if some of it feels new and unwanted.

Sadness is the most familiar and perhaps the most acceptable emotion. Weeping and feeling sad are normal and will recede with time. Grief might feel like an illness but it isn't. It's a natural process we need to go through to recover our equilibrium. It takes time and courage, but the majority of people do heal. I will now show what helps recovery, and what assistance is needed for those who do not recover naturally.

3

How to mourn

Although we all have different ways of expressing grief, there is a general consensus about what helps the process along. The first and most essential is the proactive support of family and friends. In the case of death, it is they who share in the mourning rituals that enable the bereaved to accomplish Worden's first task of grieving, which is to accept the reality of the loss.

According to Parkes, grieving people are like wounded animals in need of care and protection. Who better to give this than the people who know and love us best? Support can be practical. For instance, a death brings overwhelming practical and administrative tasks in its train which can be undertaken, at least initially, by others. It can be a blessing to have someone take over even simple things like answering the telephone, helping with finances, making meals or entertaining the children. It can be even more important just to be able to listen. Those who grieve tend to have an almost obsessive need to talk about their loss, particularly at first. Shakespeare understood this when he wrote, 'Give sorrow words: the grief that does not speak Whispers the o'er-fraught heart and bids it break.' Talking helps us makes sense of what's happened. Generally, it is easier to do this with people who share and understand our grief than with strangers.

'I couldn't have got through without my friends,' Michaela told me.

They literally held me up. First, family and friends came to stay to help with the phone and the arrangements. Some close Indian friends arrived unbidden just to sit with me in quiet sympathy. That was very moving. After a few weeks, when my sons went home, I knew there were friends whom I could ring day or night if I needed. I appreciate so much all they have done for me. At this stage, more than two years on, you start fearing loneliness and that the phone will stop ringing so it is comforting to have friends who still keep in touch.

I interviewed Simon and Jenny several years after their oldest son was killed in a flying accident. They told me how fortified they had been by the support of family and friends as well as all those who sent flowers and letters. Simon was comforted by the pastor and by the surprising number of people who told him of their own losses. 'When I hear of parents who have lost children I feel a close sense of identity, almost as if we were members of the same club.'

When Helen's husband committed suicide she found out who her real friends were.

> They were the ones who helped me to survive the first winter of despair. Since that time I have dropped a good dozen of friends who couldn't or wouldn't show support in helping me stay alive. It was an easy choice. A great solace were the letters that I got; the more they celebrated my husband's accomplishments and character the more I cherished them. When some of his friends showed anger that he could do such a terrible thing to me I cringed and held a grudge.

Grief is lightened by being shared. A friend described this to me in a beautiful way.

> I looked around at all the people who had come to my son's funeral and I felt that each person there had taken a little piece of grief away from me, leaving me lighter by the end. It was a strange and wonderful feeling.

From my interviews I have learnt what the majority of bereaved people need from their friends. They appreciate being contacted right away, even if not much is said at this time. Letters of sympathy which can be read and re-read give much comfort. They are grateful to those who keep in touch with visits and invitations after the initial support has faded and when loneliness may have intensified. During this time of indecision it is not helpful to be told, 'Don't hesitate to ring if you need anything.' It is easier to be offered practical assistance or specific invitations. It can be hurtful if friends stop talking about the dead person. Mutually recalled memories are important, especially on anniversaries and special occasions.

From the beginning of time societies have developed rituals (often very elaborate, as in ancient Egypt) to provide a structured way in which family and friends can express their grief. However much these vary between cultures and religions, they have the same overall purpose: to emphasize the reality of the death; to honour the dead person; to allow for community participation; and to help the bereaved to process their grief so that they can move on. Christian funerals, which are still the majority in Britain, can vary according to denomination, but most churches have specific funeral services during which there are hymns, readings and a eulogy. In contrast to Victorian times there is no prescribed mourning period during which formal condolences are made, but it is growing more common to follow a private funeral with a more public memorial service which provides the opportunity for friends and colleagues to celebrate the life of the deceased.

In the Jewish religion the burial service takes place in the cemetery, where a eulogy is given by the rabbi and an ancient prayer called the Kaddish is recited. Afterwards everyone returns home to eat a meal of consolation prepared by friends. Shiva, which starts on the day of the funeral and lasts for a week, is the time when the bereaved members of the family sit at home to receive all those who come to convey their condolences. Official mourning lasts for 11 months during which the Kaddish is recited daily. At the end of this period the tombstone is unveiled.

Hindus in Britain cannot carry out certain of the rituals – for example, scattering the ashes in the Ganges – which are set out in the holy texts. However, government agencies are making more efforts to meet their religious needs. I saw a delightful ceremony on television of a Hindu funeral party that went out in a boat to scatter ashes on the River Soar. They did this to the sound of bells and chanting.

The Buddhist ceremonies that took place in Thailand after the Tsunami disaster must have brought solace to the survivors. Groups of monks recited prayers to calm and bless the spirits of those who had suffered violent deaths.

Muslims bury their dead in ceremonies that emphasize respectful simplicity. The official mourning period is only three days, during which people visit the family to offer condolences. This does not mean that grief can only be felt for three days. On the contrary, according to the Prophet Muhammad, tears are a *rahma* placed by God in the hearts of men, and God has mercy on those who show compassion. *Rahma* is a word that means both mercy and compassion. So weeping for the dead shows that a person can feel compassion or empathy and is part of God's mercy.

In contrast, a friend of mine gave me a description of an Anglican funeral that was more in the stiff-upper-lip tradition.

> When my father died, we arranged a funeral for family only as quickly as possible. The service was taken by an unknown priest in an ugly crematorium. None of us gave a eulogy or a reading. We just hadn't considered it. The priest did his best but he hadn't a clue what my father was like. Apart from the odd snivel we were all very self-controlled. When a button was pushed and the coffin slid between curtains, presumably (but who knows?) to the fire at the other end, I was rather horrified by a desire to howl with laughter. There was something inappropriately hilarious, too, about the way we were hustled out in half an hour to make way for the next service. We walked away and never returned. I don't know what happened to the ashes.

When I asked what he would do if he had his time again he said,

> I would have delayed the funeral to enable more people to make arrangements to attend it. In fact, I wouldn't have a cremation at all. I have become quite allergic to them. I think burials in churchyards are more natural and beautiful. I would have male relatives rather than gloomy undertakers carry in the coffin. Even if the priest was a stranger, children and grandchildren and friends could do the readings. It would be so comforting to have an inscribed headstone which my children, and in due course theirs, could visit if they wanted. If it had to be a cremation I would want to do something very special with the ashes and mark the place with an inscription. In fact, that's the one reparation I could make and I intend to do it soon.

Christian burials in Britain were not always such secular, private and plain affairs. In the nineteenth century Victorian mourning rites were elaborate. The majority of people still died at home. Straw would be laid in the street to still the noise of passing traffic. Windows and doors would be draped in black cloth. The clocks were stopped. The dead person would be laid out in an open coffin in the front room where family, friends and neighbours would come and pay their respects. On the day of the funeral the coffin would be transported on a carriage pulled by plumed black horses at a pace slow enough to allow as many people as possible to join the procession. The bereaved would wear black and lead circumscribed lives until the long period of mourning was over.

Cardinal Manning's funeral in January 1892 was the last great event of its kind in the nineteenth century and is still talked about in the Catholic community today. Manning was an ascetic and saintly Catholic convert who ended his career as a Cardinal. But no one realized how much he was revered and loved by poor and ordinary people, especially the Irish, until he died. His death evoked the most extraordinary, spontaneous and unexpected demonstration of mass emotion. *The Times* estimated that 100,000 people filed past his body as it lay in state for four days in a mansion in Victoria. His tiny bedroom was rifled of its simple possessions by visitors anxious to carry off a relic. The burial route from Victoria to Kensal Green cemetery was so crammed with spectators that the police had to fight to make a passage for the funeral cortège.

The traditional Irish wake, too, has largely been consigned to the past. The wake was the ancient custom that took place between the death and the funeral, when the body of the deceased was laid out by mourners in an open coffin in the house. Neighbours and friends would come to pay their respects and socialize while they remembered the departed person's life. Much food and drink was consumed, and in the old days there would be storytelling, singing, dancing, music and card-playing.

It was partly because so many people died in the two world wars, at a time when resources were limited, that funerals and mourning rituals in Great Britain and Ireland were cut back to basics. Bereaved relatives learnt to control their expressions of grief, at least in public, because there was pressure on them to get back to coping with the difficult conditions of everyday life as soon as possible. Today, the business of dying has been largely taken out of the hands of the family by professionals in welfare, local government and medicine. Those present when we draw our last breath are as likely to be nurses as members of the family. Our bodies will be laid out by hospital staff and removed to the hospital mortuary as soon as possible, before being transferred to a funeral home where under-takers will take charge of further arrangements. You could almost say that all the relatives need to do is to look at the price list of coffins and choose a suitable date for a funeral service.

Some people are making imaginative efforts to personalize mourning rituals. An increasingly popular alternative to traditional burials and cremations are those in specifically dedicated woodland or nature reserve burial grounds. The Natural Death Centre helps people to organize these D-I-Y green burials. It is even legal now to have a private burial in the grounds of your own home. However, this cannot be done without proper registration and various permissions from agencies and the local authority. It is also important to think through the implications of selling or moving house in the future, because once a body has been buried it may not be removed without proper authority.

With the assistance of humanist organizations, it is possible to arrange burials for the non-religious who live by moral principles based on reason and respect. The only humanist funeral I attended was very dignified. An officiant led the ceremony, which was held in a country cemetery. Friends and family members celebrated the life of the dead man with stories and readings. The cheerful drinks party that followed felt perfectly appropriate.

Rituals enabled Michaela to be proactive in her own grief process.

The priest in my local church was fantastic and went far beyond the call of duty. Everything he did was right, not just at the time but afterwards when we had long and inspiring conversations together. He was wise and understanding as well as practical. He helped me with all the arrangements that followed my husband's death. I realize, looking back, that in addition to the conventional rituals I invented some for myself. First there was the funeral, of course. This was just for family and very close friends. Our Indian friends had sent two phials of oil for love and remem-brance that the vicar found a way of using in the Anglican funeral service. Five weeks later we had a memorial service in a bigger church. Friends and work colleagues gave eulogies about him that moved me profoundly. It wasn't until six months later that we had a ceremony for the scattering of the ashes. I wasn't sure how best to keep them in the meantime, so the vicar stored them for me below the altar in the church. The ashes were scattered in a beautiful garden where we made an inscription. It is nearby so that it is easy to visit and just sit in contemplation. I kept back some of the ashes and had a ceremony all to myself in the mountains where we had had so many happy times together. I see now how important all these rituals have been.

Simon and Jenny also created their own rituals.

We needed to go to the scene of the plane accident. It was necessary to see the wreckage and the bloodstains, not to make it more real but because it was the place where our son had last been. It was a sort of spiritual communion. I picked up sticks and stones – just small objects that will always be precious. His plane crashed in a beautiful place. We put a rock there. We had a small and simple cremation service right away and later a church service on the island where we spend our holidays. We have created a memorial garden for him there. The ashes are buried near the sea at the bottom of our garden. We have marked it with rocks and some sculptured birds. It is so comforting to be able to see him every day.

Simon and Jenny have found lovely ways with which to honour and remember their son. Creating a suitable headstone or inscription is a worthwhile task that can involve everyone in the family. Harriet Frazer, who has created an association called Memorials by Artists, described in *Crusenews* what had motivated her.

It is now 15 years since I had the idea for Memorials by Artists. This was following the tragic death by suicide of my 26-year-old stepdaughter, Sophie. The commissioning of her memorial was one of the most difficult things our family had to do ... and yet the outcome was so positive. The collaboration we had with the memorial maker to produce a unique, well-designed and beautiful memorial to Sophie helped us greatly in our grief.

Visiting a grave, marking an anniversary, lighting candles, saying prayers or revisiting special places are private rituals that can be repeated for years. Mourning rituals are deeply comforting and provide identifiable milestones along the road to recovery.

4
Helping grief along

Worden's second task is to work through the pain of grief. This means accepting the necessity of pain and then finding creative ways of expressing it. Writer and psychoanalyst Robin Skynner defines grief as follows,

> Grief is when you accept the loss. You don't shrink from the natural suffering it causes you and you're concerned more about the person who has died than about yourself. You let the pain act on you, let it change you. Then it forces you to let go.

In *The Rebecca Notebook*, Daphne du Maurier too urges us to confront grief head-on. 'The pain will come in waves, some days worse than others, for no apparent reason. Accept the pain. Do not suppress it. Never attempt to hide grief from yourself.' She promises that little by little the bereaved 'will find new strength, new vision born of the very pain and loneliness which seem at first impossible to master'.

Writing can prove a lifeline. C. S. Lewis' journal was not simply a 'defence against total collapse, a safety-valve', but has encouraged thousands of readers throughout the world. Alison Wertheimer wrote her important book *A Special Scar* after the suicide of her sister. Blake Morrison wrote *And When Did You Last See Your Father?* after the death of his larger-than-life parent.

The book that moved me most is entitled *Before I Say Goodbye*, by Ruth Picardie. This spirited South African journalist died of cancer at the age of 32. From the moment she got the diagnosis until near the end, she shared the progress of her terminal illness and all the emotions that went with it with the readers of *The Observer* 'Life' section. How she raged and sorrowed. She was completely honest and had a mordant sense of humour. She did mad and frivolous things and did not give up hope until there was no hope left. Her columns had a dramatic effect on her readers, some of whom wrote in to sympathize, commiserate, advise and encourage, and most of all to share their own personal stories of grief with her.

A few of the letters reproduced in Ruth's book give us a flavour of the chord she struck in the lives of so many. A woman who had just ended treatment for cancer wrote, 'I hope that you are surrounded by people who love you, and who can support and hold your hostile and despairing feelings, and also be with you when a little bit of joy comes creeping in, against all the odds.' Another reader recommended brick-throwing as helpful. A doctor from Glasgow told her of his intention to use her writings as essential reading for his medical students embarking on a career in hospice medicine. 'I can only send my thanks for your diary and my best wishes, for what they are worth, to your family. I, for one, though I will never meet you, will miss you when you go.'

But it is not just professional writers who turn to the pen. All sorts of people who did not think themselves the slightest bit literary have found that writing things down gives them a better handle on their tumultuous emotions. Writing helps us to make better sense of events and provides more of a sense of control at a time of helplessness. And perhaps much later, it can give us a sense of achievement to look back and see that some progress has been made along the pathway of grief. Michaela kept a commonplace book in which she noted down quotations and thoughts that comforted her. She lost her concentration and couldn't read books but found comfort in reading poetry. Now, two years on, she is ready to tackle the letters of condolence which were sent to her. She is looking forward to re-reading them and answering each one.

The raw and powerful emotions triggered by grief can be channelled into any creative activity. Jean Parker is well aware of how much sculpting helped her, but had not counted on the effect her *Bald Statements* had on other people. Since she created them they have been exhibited in many different settings. She is frequently being asked to give talks and workshops for doctors, nurses and other professionals involved with bereavement. She has also been commissioned to make memorials for people who have died. Another artist whose grief found expression in art was the great Surrealist Belgian painter René Magritte, who died in 1967. When he was 14 his mother walked out of the house during the night and was found washed up in a river, with her white nightdress tangled around her face. The image of a woman posed like a statue with her head hidden in a white shroud is one that he often repeated. We do not need to be trained artists to use pencil, paint, wood or other materials to express emotions. Traditionally in the United States women have gathered together to commemorate sad or happy events by sewing patchwork quilts or making embroideries.

A popular way of dealing positively with grief is to turn it into a vehicle for helping others. Self-help groups by definition consist of people who have been through common experiences. The bereaved derive strength from helping others who are at a different stage in the grief process. Others raise money for medical research, hospital equipment and the treatment of rare diseases. Many charities have been created as a direct result of someone's death. The Suzy Lamplugh Trust is a good example of this. The charity was established in 1986 by Diana Lamplugh when her daughter Suzy, who was an estate agent, disappeared while working. Her body has never been found and she is presumed murdered. The Lamplugh Trust has grown into the leading authority on personal safety. Its role is to minimize the damage caused to individuals and society by aggression in all its forms, whether on transport, at home or in schools and colleges.

The Zito Trust is another well-known charity that was set up as a direct result of a tragic death. When Christopher Clunis, who was suffering from schizophrenia, stabbed Jonathan Zito to death in 1994, Jonathan's widow Jayne set up this mental health charity, which seeks to highlight issues relating to mental illness and the care of those affected by it. Cruse, Samaritans, Survivors of Bereavement by Suicide and countless other bodies were all started on a small scale by volunteers. The hospice movement, the Royal Marsden Hospital and Great Ormond Street Hospital for Children rely heavily for funds from people who have lost family members and want to give something back to the institutions that cared for them.

After the Paddington train crash in 1999 when two trains crashed, killing 31 people and injuring hundreds, some of the survivors formed a support group. They spent five years fighting for compensation and safety improvements. The Paddington Survivors Group learnt so much about post-traumatic stress, compensation and safety that they now want to offer themselves as a resource to aid future crash victims. They also want to keep up the pressure on government to improve train safety. This seems such a good way of turning tragedy into a resource for others.

Worden's third task, to adjust to the new environment, takes effort and courage. The passage of time is an important element for this task. When we are suffering we naturally want the pain to go away and so are impatient and unrealistic about how long it will take. Men in particular, I find, are anxious to get over their feelings and feel normal again. To help people get a more realistic sense of time I ask them to think how long it takes to recover from a broken leg or a heart by-pass operation. I also ask them to think of friends or relatives who have had some grievous loss and recall how long it took for them to get over it. I remind them that however much the outer world is urging them to get back to normal, the inner world of emotions has its own time scale and rhythm for healing. 'Going with the flow' sounds trite but it fits well with the grief process. The symptoms of grief should gradually diminish over six to 18 months. Two and a half years on, Michaela says that, while she feels stronger, 'I think I feel more depressed because I have to face up to the realization that I will be leading the rest of my life as a single person.' Simon admits that 'the intensity does pass but grief still hits me unexpectedly in all sort of ways. And in a way I want to hold on to my grief. I am afraid of forgetting my son.'

One of the most important but most difficult things to do after a death or major loss is to do nothing at all. Taking big decisions when we are at our most physically and mentally debilitated is not wise. Our judgement tends to be impaired and we are frequently operating in a context of fearfulness. This is not the time to be leaving the country, moving house, selling possessions, changing the children's schools or starting new relationships. Yet these decisions are often forced on us by financial necessity or other pressures and we are left to cope the best we can.

Whenever and wherever it is possible, though, it is a good idea to keep things going as before. I will show in a later chapter how important this is for children. Routines supply a modicum of discipline and can keep us from going to pieces. Jenny was helped by the need to keep life as normal as possible for her two other children. 'We simply could not go into decline and we didn't. We needed to go on celebrating Christmas and organizing the summer holidays. Work was essential to me. I don't know what I would have done without it.' Work is a place where we can feel needed and valued. It provides a reason for getting up in the morning and it protects against total loneliness, though full commitment cannot and should not be expected for some months at least, otherwise work will become a stress and not a support.

Turbulent emotions are wayward and do not feel amenable to control, but physically we can really help ourselves. It is tempting, when we are in a state of shock and sorrow, to neglect ourselves. Nights are disturbed and mental and physical exhaustion sets in. It is easy to let go when we feel we have lost our reason for living. Why bother to eat properly, or look good? What is the point in exercising? What's wrong with a drink, or two or three, if it numbs our feelings? It may feel counter-intuitive, but taking care of our bodies will help to heal our minds. Michaela felt that the efforts she made to look after herself really paid off.

> The physical side was easier to tackle than my emotions. It was the one thing I felt I had some control over. My doctor was very wise. He told me not to worry about taking sleeping pills because I wouldn't be able to cope without sleep. He told me to pick at food throughout the day if I couldn't eat a meal. I made sure that I kept up a regular exercise regime. I know this did me a great deal of good. It forces you to focus on something else and was a distraction from my sad thoughts, as well as making me feel healthier.

Counselling, while not mandatory, can be extremely helpful. Some people turn to counselling because they feel they cannot impose on their friends any longer; would prefer an impartial listener; or have no one else to whom they can turn. Experience in the hospice movement has shown the value of counselling families before the death of someone with cancer. And all the experts agree that should people get stuck in the grief process, therapy is necessary. Many bereaved people want to talk to a specially trained bereavement counsellor. Self-help groups have a similar appeal. There are support groups for people who have lost a child, for anyone bereaved by the death of a same-sex partner or friends, and for people bereaved by suicide and violent death. After national disasters support groups get created and continue for as long as there are people who feel the need to attend them. Support of this kind can be tremendously helpful and a list is provided at the end of the book. The Internet is also proving a popular medium of communication. Adolescents, in particular, sometimes find it easier to express their emotions with a sympathetic stranger in a virtual chat room than with people they know.

In the context of Worden's fourth task, how do we know when we have completed the emotional process and moved on? Grief feels unique to each person. I do not believe that we all need to go through the whole gamut of emotions to get better. Those who do not manifest strong emotions should not be forced to do so. In my opinion it is not how we grieve but whether we recover that counts. And we only have to look around us to see how we can and do recover. Most of us have greater inner and outer resources upon which to draw than we ever imagined. Michaela realizes she is recovering because the effort she had to make to keep distracted, motivated and optimistic is becoming more automatic. One sign of recovery is to be able to participate fully in life without forgetting or rejecting the person or experience that meant so much. Simon and Jenny now have a grandson who is named after their dead son. This is a great joy to them, though they are sensitive about not investing him with their son's identity. This is just one of the many ways they keep his memory alive in a natural way. Helen, whose husband committed suicide, told me that she did not think her tragedy had changed her personality,

> other than I think I've acquired a greater understanding. Maybe I am more generous in my judgements. And maybe I'll know a little better now that there's some strength to be counted on. Last but not least, love never dies. My new partner and I often talk about my husband and all survivors should have or take this privilege.

Michaela is strengthened by her belief that her life is richer because her husband was in it.

5

Complicated grief

Painful though grieving may be, the majority of us do get through the process. The signs that we are healing and moving on may be almost imperceptible. We begin to laugh and joke again. We get through a day without crying. We can read a book and remember its contents. We can listen to music without making painful associations. We are less introspective. We have enough energy to do things for other people. Decisions become easier to make. We begin to make plans and look forward. Feelings of hope re-emerge. In short, we are starting to reinvest in life again. But there are individuals who get stuck in what the experts term complicated or abnormal grief.

I dare say we all know someone we think of as terminally grief-stricken. I certainly have two friends in this category. One is a woman who was widowed when she was 40. Although she goes through the motions and makes a huge effort to be positive and active she seems permanently surrounded by an aura of depression. Thirty years on, this woman still talks about her husband's death as if it happened yesterday. The other is a man whose wife had poor health for years before she died. He's got money, charm and good looks. Women find him very attractive, but he makes it clear that intimacy is not for him because his heart is broken. Both these individuals are going through the motions of living, but in essence have withdrawn a large part of themselves.

What other signs might indicate to us that someone we know is stuck in grief? Complaints of sickness and physical symptoms may provide a clue. These are normal at the beginning but should not persist for years or even months. On several occasions doctors have referred patients to me for emotional work if they can find no physical explanation for aches, pains, panic attacks or fatigue and suspect that the ailments may be psychosomatic.

Another sign is if someone is drinking too much, taking drugs or becoming over-reliant on tranquillizers. To want to blunt strong emotions is a natural reaction, but if substance abuse becomes an addiction it brings all sorts of attendant problems in its train. Meanwhile, the grieving doesn't get done. Addiction is a difficult problem to deal with because it is so often denied. And the accident, death or whatever started the substance abuse serves as an excuse to continue it. Professional help should be sought for those who manifestly can't stop by themselves. Addiction counsellors tell me that therapy with their clients invariably brings up repressed emotions for past losses that have been buried or denied. Once these have been addressed, recovery is possible.

It is fairly obvious if someone gets stuck in an angry, bitter and blaming stage and cannot move on. Take, for instance, the case of the managing director of a business who is being pursued in the courts by a disgruntled employee, dismissed for incompetence ten years ago. This is aptly called 'grievous litigation'. As we have seen, it is quite normal to feel anger and be able to express it after a loss, especially if negligence or incompetence has been involved. These negative feelings, however, should abate after a few months. It is not normal to be actively holding a grudge ten years after the event. I do on occasion work with people who have been experiencing furious and bitter feelings for years – as a result of a divorce, for example. When such cases crop up in my therapy room, as they sometimes do, I leave the divorce on one side and focus on early histories because that is where the wound usually resides.

Long-term depression is quite a common reaction to severe loss. Depressed feelings are to be expected in the aftermath of a loss or shock. It is normal for people to weep, to sleep badly, to eat too much or too little, to feel listless and to lose hope. But if these feelings persist for more than six months and involve serious loss of self-esteem, then a doctor should be consulted. Social isolation is another symptom of depression. If friends or family begin to realize that someone has stopped socializing, or is in a state of neglect, alarm bells should start ringing. Sometimes people feel so overpowered and helpless that they contemplate suicide. A passive feeling of just not seeing the point of going on is one thing; actively considering ending life is quite another, and professional help should be sought.

Frenetic and inappropriate activity can also be a sign of dysfunction. Again, this can be normal for a short time, but becomes worrying if it goes on for too long. We've all probably seen examples of grieving individuals who become promiscuous, or fill their lives with restless socializing, work or travel. People will go to extraordinary lengths to avoid pain, loneliness and sadness. In relation to the loss-orientation and restoration-orientation model of grief mentioned earlier, these people are rushing into recovery mode at the expense of allowing themselves to experience their pain and sadness more fully. But these feelings have a way of coming out eventually.

As I explained earlier, guilt may be a necessary and appropriate reaction, but it can also be a heavy burden that stops people from moving on. I have particular sympathy for people who suffer what we now call 'survivor guilt'. This phenomenon has been much discussed in relation to Jews and others who survived internment in concentration camps where the majority of inmates died. Many survivors of September 11 experienced similar feelings. After the Tsunami deluge I heard some survivors who had lost their entire families declare that they wished they had perished too.

Before I even became a therapist I was struck by the case of Apsley Cherry-Garrard, the Antarctic explorer who suffered from survivor guilt. Known to his friends as Cherry, he was only 24 when he joined Captain Scott's ill-fated expedition to the Antarctic in 1910. In the following year, Scott made the final push to the South Pole with four companions while the rest of the party stayed at base camp. Scott and his companions perished on the way back from the Pole, which the Norwegian explorer Amundsen had reached before him. They had run out of food and fuel 11 miles from the last depot, which Cherry had been responsible for provisioning for their return journey. Cherry was in the party that finally found the dead men, frozen in a tent. He suffered from a terrible feeling of guilt for not having been able to save them. Mixed up in this guilt were feelings of anger against Scott, whose misjudgements he felt had led to the deaths of his two best friends. He suffered from depression and ulcerative colitis for years afterwards. Cherry belatedly found some comfort from sessions with a psychiatrist who had some understanding of the ordeals he had endured.

The problem of guilt can be dealt with in a number of ways. Talking to a therapist, informed outsider or pastor can help those burdened with guilt to gain a wider and less personally focused perspective. It may need someone else to point out that there were wider influences and factors involved in an event for which the person is taking so much responsibility. Those with religious beliefs may be able to hand the guilt over to God, or put it in a wider spiritual context. If forgiveness from God is not acceptable, the guilty person will need to find forgiveness from within. I find that people who blame themselves tend to be very self-critical. So I ask them to consider the possibility that they might be as compassionate to themselves as they would be to others.

The following extra factors can make grieving more complicated: if the loss is very sudden or unexpected; if it involves violence or horror; if the relationship that preceded it was conflict-ridden or over-dependent; if practical problems lead to the suppression of feelings; or if it comes on top of a series of other losses.

During a long terminal illness, partners can get close, make amends, plan for the future and say goodbye in a mutually satisfying way. When death does occur it makes some sense, however hateful the process has been. On the other hand, those who suffer from sudden and unexpected death are in shock and often have difficulty in accepting the reality of the loss, suffer from feelings of self-reproach and despair and lose their trust in the world. If something so bad has happened once, why not again?

If a sudden death takes place in horrific circumstances, such as happens with suicide, homicide or in a disaster like a train crash, then normal grief can be compounded by post-traumatic stress disorder (PTSD). This occurs when the trauma is so severe that the victim remains in a permanent state of alertness and arousal. The symptoms may manifest as panic attacks, irritability, depression, anxious thoughts, flashbacks, insomnia and nightmares. In more severe cases, victims of a trauma might experience emotional or physical numbness or detachment from reality. Although PTSD was originally diagnosed among military personnel, it is now considered to be a more common phenomenon. In a memoir entitled *Lucky*, remarkable for its searing candour, the American writer Alice Sebold recounts the trauma of being brutally raped and beaten up in her freshman year in college. Long after she and her family considered that she should have got over her grief, she was still suffering from insomnia, depression and anxiety. The feelings were so uncomfortable that she numbed herself with drink, drugs and unsatisfactory relationships. It was only several years later, when PTSD was diagnosed, that she got appropriate help. It is very important to consult a specialist if such symptoms persist because there are various treatments on offer, including exposure therapy and hypnosis.

One might suppose that the happier a relationship is, the more intense will be the grief if it ends. In fact, research shows the opposite. Relationships that are conflict-ridden, overly dependent or troubled are more likely to lead to the survivors experiencing unyielding grief. They do not just mourn the relationship, but the lack of one. They have fewer happy memories to internalize. Insecure attachments in their own childhood might be compounding their feelings of loss. Queen Victoria, dubbed 'the widow of Windsor', is always quoted as an example of someone who indulged in morbid grieving. After 22 years of marriage which she remembered as idyllic, the Queen ostentatiously mourned Prince Albert for the rest of her life. A photograph of his corpse was hung above the unoccupied side of her bed. His clothes were laid out each day and nothing in his rooms was allowed to be touched. At the time she was criticized for withdrawing from public life and doubts about her sanity were publicly expressed. Queen Victoria had been overly dependent on Albert. She had relied heavily on him in her public role and in the private management of their children. When he died she felt unable to undertake the magnitude of her tasks without him. Another sign of the Queen's abnormal grief was the degree to which she idealized Albert. In retrospect it seemed that he could do no wrong. In fact, no one is perfect and putting the deceased on a pedestal is not a natural or healthy response to death.

The grief process can be skewed by outside events and practical pressures. Death and divorce in particular can lead to drastic changes in lifestyles. Colin came to see me professionally 12 years after his wife died, leaving him with two small children. He was having commitment problems in a new relationship. The therapy quickly switched from his present problems to his wife's death. Before this happened their roles had been clearly defined. He had gone out to work and she looked after the children at home. Within a week, his whole world had been turned upside down. He gave up his job and took on the care of the children. He worked as hard as he could from home after the children had gone to bed. He made a decision that he would not disturb the status quo for his children by having a new relationship until they had left home.

All my energy went into caring for them. It was a constant learning curve and I never seem to have had time for myself. I can't even remember missing my wife, which seems strange to think about because I was devastated by her death.

Colin's case is a good example of someone whose feelings of grief were put on hold while he got to grips with practicalities and the necessity of learning new skills. If people don't get the chance to feel the sadness and pain at the time, the feelings get buried. They might resurface unexpectedly or get triggered by a new loss, bringing intense feelings to the fore.

Financial problems, fights for compensation or disputes about inheritance can also disrupt the normal grief process. In my experience, too, the discovery of secrets after death complicates grief. Certain revelations can be destabilizing because they destroy the preconceived ideas of how things were: the existence of other significant relationships, the existence of previous children, and knowledge that a parent is not the natural parent. It is hard to have to readjust the picture and understanding of the person you have just lost on top of everything else.

The grieving process can be intensified if someone has previously suffered a series of losses in their lives. In such cases, the previous losses get triggered and the feelings get compounded. Ben came to see me after the break-up of a four-year relationship. Rationally, he had known that the relationship wasn't right. He considered that he and his partner brought out the worst in each other. Nevertheless, he felt devastated by its ending. He wasn't eating or sleeping and was finding it hard to get to work. As we talked about previous losses in his life, it transpired that he had suffered two for which he had expressed no sorrow at the time. His father left the family for another woman when he was 11. His mother was so destabilized by this that she became mentally ill. Ben became the steady little carer. At the same time he had to get himself to school. Because his mother got so upset he didn't talk about his father, whose visits ceased shortly after the divorce. Young though he was, there was nobody to talk to him about his sadness and loss. Therapy gave him permission to grieve retrospectively. Eventually, he was able to tell his mother of his suffering as a boy and he became reconciled with his father. Consequently, he began to have trust in his own relationships.

What helps those of us who get stuck in grief? First, it might be revealing to ask ourselves a few basic questions. Is grief keeping us from getting on with our lives? Have we become so introspective that we cannot think of anything but our own sorrow and loss? Are we avoiding taking decisions that involve change? Is grief alienating or separating us from friends and relatives? If the answer to these questions is yes, then we need to make positive efforts to climb out of the slough of despond and self-pity. Some people are born with optimistic strength; others have to work to develop it. Start by setting small but realistic goals for reconnecting with other people. Local libraries have lists of organizations in need of volunteers. We have already learnt how helping others helps to process individual grief. Another way to move from profound introspection to a wider perspective is to hand grief over to a higher power. Over and over I have heard how in sorrow people have turned to God again, or found strength and solace in a new religion. Grief is absorbed through spiritual enlightenment.

If these paths are not appealing, it is worth creating a private ritual to facilitate the letting go of grief. Pouring out feelings (positive and negative) in a letter to the loved one can be cathartic. The letter can then be burnt or buried, or left on the grave. It might also be locked up in a drawer for re-reading on an anniversary. Something similar can be done by making up a box of special items associated with the deceased and then burying or putting aside the box to symbolize the packaging up of the grief in a way that is freeing. Grieving can take up so much psychic and physical energy that it can be extremely helpful to devise a rationing ritual. This involves making a pact with oneself to get on with enjoyment and living in exchange for a designated time on a daily or weekly basis when grief and tears are permitted. Someone told me that she kept her grieving for bath time. Somehow it comforted her to watch her tears becoming one with the water in the bath.

The benefit of physical exercise has already been mentioned, but it is worth emphasizing. We widely accept that taking exercise is good for our physical health. It is not so widely understood that it is good for our mental health too. The fitter we are the better we feel about ourselves. Taking exercise is a way of socializing and making connections with others. It raises our spirits because we have less time to brood on negative thoughts. Most importantly, it has a direct chemical and biological effect on the mind by releasing increased levels of endorphins and enkephalins – the chemicals that relieve pain and promote feelings of well-being.

If nothing seems to work and depression does not lift, it would be wise to consult a doctor or psychiatrist who can prescribe anti-depressant medication. While pills will not obliterate grief, they can restore the chemical balance in the body. With increased energy and concentration it becomes easier to process emotions. Talking to a therapist or pastor can be helpful. These professionals can provide a contained and safe place for people to discharge their painful emotions. They can help to provide reality checks and information, especially when dealing with guilt and self-reproach. They can help people to get in touch with resources and self-confidence that have all but disappeared. They might generate a spiritual dimension that leads to tranquillity. They can help to grow hope, without which people cannot recover. Joining a therapy group or self-help group can be extremely helpful. Going on a retreat can be a healing experience too. These are often organized by religious groups and offer time and space for contemplation and discussion.

6

Losses

Most of the individuals, couples or families who come to see me for therapy are grieving a loss of one sort or another. Starting at the beginning of the life cycle, I shall describe some of the losses, such as infertility, miscarriage, stillbirth, adoption and divorce, that can cause grief in everyday life, and how people have coped with them.

Infertility is a much greater cause for grief than those of us who have not experienced it realize. There is a very strong age-old social presumption in most communities throughout the world that when a couple is formed, children should follow in the natural course of events. Couples who have made a positive choice to remain childless are subject to careless remarks, like 'When are you going to try for a baby?' or 'What a shame you haven't got children. Who will look after you in your old age?' Such remarks are doubly hurtful for couples who want a baby but find they can't have one.

A feeling of failure is commonplace. An infertile woman feels that she has failed in a primary task and possibly let down her own parents if they are longing to be grandparents. 'It makes me feel so inadequate not being able to have a baby. You know, some people who don't know how hard I've tried, imply that I am selfish not to have any children,' Mary told me. 'All my contemporaries seem to be breeding like rabbits. Although part of me feels glad for them, another part hates them. And when I hear of someone having an abortion the sense of injustice is overwhelming.' An infertile man may experience feelings of shame, embarrassment and failure. 'I feel very responsible for the fact that we can't have children,' explains James, 'but I don't like the thought of using another man's sperm. My wife is very supportive of me now but I do wonder whether she will blame me when we are older.'

Infertility is not an easy subject to share with others, so feelings of isolation are common. Recent developments in assisted reproductive technology (ART) offer hope to the infertile, but in vitro fertilization (IVF) and other treatments, involving large doses of hormone stimulants, are invasive, stressful and expensive. In fact, I have known of several couples whose relationships have broken apart as a direct consequence of the strain of IVF treatment. Years of treatment can end in failure. And failure means rethinking a whole way of life. 'I've wanted a baby for so long and so hard it has affected all my relationships, which have broken up. I don't think I will be reconciled to being barren until I reach the menopause, and then I will probably always be sad.' Mary is still evidently in the throes of grieving and is not yet able to contemplate other options. But I have worked with infertile couples who have accepted their loss and gone on to adopt or foster; who have concentrated on careers; or who have become important figures in the lives of other people's children.

Adoption for couples who can't have children is a most rewarding option, but the pain and loss that underlie it often go unacknowledged. In the adoption triangle adoptees have lost the parents who gave them life. In many cases adoptive parents have lost the chance of having their own children, and the birth parents have lost the children they brought into the world. A great deal is expected from adoptive parents. At the beginning they may have spent frustrating and humiliating years trying to conceive children of their own. They have to undergo a unique process of scrutiny and assessment before being allowed to become parents. A sense of being on trial is combined with doubts as to their entitlement to someone else's child.

Children who were adopted as babies and have only scant or no knowledge of their birth parents can experience identity problems, which is not surprising if we consider how the natural flow of their lives suffered a disjunction at the time of their birth. They often suffer a sense of being and feeling different. Therapists have long been aware that some adopted adults suffer from a sense of rootlessness and a fear of failure and rejection. I believe that birth mothers suffer the worst grief of all because it tends to be unacknowledged and unresolved. The majority of mothers who relinquished their babies, especially in the past, felt forced to do so because of difficult circumstances. Even if they never hear about these children again, they never forget them. The subject may be too difficult and painful to share with others and becomes repressed grief that may be compounded by feelings of guilt and regret. Many adoptees search for their birth parents and succeed in finding them. Birth parents too sometimes try to find their children. Today, we are more aware of the needs of everyone in the adoption triangle and try to meet them more sensitively than we have in the past. We also know that if the natural feelings of loss and sorrow can be acknowledged and worked through, the adoptive relationships will be strengthened.

If we are trying for a baby and manage to conceive, we regard the pregnancy as a matter for joy and optimism. As the days pass, the baby in the womb acquires characteristics and a name. It is a real blow if a miscarriage occurs. What might be viewed as just a cluster of cells or a foetus to outsiders is a baby – their baby – in the minds of the expectant parents. The emotional investment in this baby can be as great at three months as at nine. If a late miscarriage occurs, the baby is an unmistakable physical presence. A miscarriage can feel like a death to the parents, though others, even the doctors involved, seldom see it like that.

It is very difficult to mourn the death of someone who was never born. There is no body to bury, no funeral, no rite to ease the passage. Unless someone has experienced the pain of miscarriage it is hard to understand how it feels. The commiseration of friends tends to be brief and sometimes insensitive because there is nothing to show for it. 'You can have another go,' or 'Maybe it's a blessing in disguise if there was something wrong with it,' or 'It's nature's way,' are typical remarks. Yet for the sad and disappointed parents there is much to grieve for, and a lot be fearful about. Was this my fault? Is there something wrong with me? Was this my last chance to have a baby? Will a miscarriage happen again? The first few months of a new pregnancy can be fraught with anxiety.

The Multiple Births Foundation booklet *When a Twin or Triplet Dies* reminds us how parents who lose a twin or triplet in a miscarriage or at birth feel that their loss is underestimated. Family, friends and professionals tend to focus on the surviving child and encourage parents to do the same, not understanding that parents have a constant reminder of their loss in the survivor. Remarks like 'It would have been hard to cope with three babies,' or 'How lucky you are still to have one,' do not help. It is almost impossible to grieve for a baby who has died at the same time as caring for and rejoicing in the survivor.

One of the unique difficulties for those with a surviving twin or triplet is that, because it makes it easier for people not to have to talk about the dead baby, the survivor tends to receive all the attention and comments. In some cases, the infant who has died is not even mentioned. This can be very hurtful.

It can help to talk to others who have been through a similar loss. Using the helplines of relevant organizations can be a first step. If a foetus is sufficiently developed to be delivered in hospital, a proper burial can be organized with the help of the hospital staff. Otherwise, couples have found it very helpful to organize their own rituals or memorials at home or in a beautiful place. Church and religious communities can be supportive if they are involved. I do not know a single woman who has had a miscarriage who has not named the baby, at least for herself, and who does not remember the anniversary of the loss.

Not everyone will have sympathy or understanding for women who choose to have abortions, but there is loss involved nevertheless. It is hard to talk openly about a voluntary termination. Because it is a choice there is an implication that the consequences need to be borne without complaint or fuss. Yet a termination often does not feel voluntary to one of the partners and tends to be loaded with shame and guilt. There is a tendency to minimize the significance of what is being done and reduce it to a simple medical procedure. In my experience the pain of a termination is seldom dealt with at the time and so is likely to come out years later when triggered by another loss, or if something goes wrong with a later pregnancy.

But abortion can be handled in a creative and positive way, as I learnt from the account Jo gave me.

When I found out I was pregnant I was shocked and afraid and didn't know what to do. But I quickly got hold of as much practical information as I could from the Internet. I felt I had to do something urgently before the life inside me grew. I told my partner immediately, partly because he had the right to know and partly because I bloody well wasn't going to go through this alone. First we just shared the news and then we went for a counselling session together. It was useful because the counsellor told us there was no need to be in such a rush. The only person I told at this stage was my acupuncturist. There is shame and fear around it. And I felt shame about my relationship as well. I was embarrassed that my partner wasn't sufficiently committed to the

43

relationship to want a child. So I got into coping mode and had the procedure. I wanted everything to be flushed out and get on with life. Two months later I broke up with my partner. Then I really really cried. It triggered a huge amount for me. I also cried about my grandma who had recently died. In effect I was grieving for three losses.

Some months later I went away by myself on a sort of retreat. This helped me to come back to myself. I was able to tell more people. The termination had made me think about what I needed in my relationship and in my life. I remember standing on a hill and thanking 'the little life' and wishing it well. I had a spiritual sense that it was back in a bigger universe. Eventually together we sponsored a tree as a memorial and wrote the inscription that read 'In honour of ourselves and the little life that passed through us'. I do worry that I might not find a partner and will have missed my chance to have children and I do sometimes think of 'the little life', but without any trauma, because we parted on good terms.

Having a stillborn child or one that dies in childbirth is a very painful event. Julia Samuel, Counsellor for Paediatrics and Maternity at St Mary's Hospital, Paddington, believes that there are particular difficulties for parents who lose babies at this stage.

The point is that a mother has only known her baby internally so it is difficult to accept the reality of the loss. Take the mother, for instance, who has been anaesthetized, has a caesarean and then gives birth to a dead baby. She goes home without a cognitive memory of what happened to her. It is not encoded in her brain. For all parents who give birth to a dead baby it is helpful to create some memories of their child. It might seem like a torture but it is really helpful to wash and hold the baby, to name it and talk to it. Photos can be taken, and footprints made and a lock of hair retained. Planning a meaningful funeral will also be a great comfort.

Julia tells parents that they well might grieve for longer than they want, but offers practical suggestions for helping the process along. She understands that the desire for another baby may be strong but cautions against getting pregnant three months after the death because the new baby would then be born on the anniversary of the baby that died. Anniversaries continue to be painful. Because the trauma is held physically in the body as well as in the mind, exercise and healthy eating helps to restore a feeling of balance. Relaxation and diversion are to be recommended. Making up a memory box and keeping a journal can help. She knows that there will be a high level of anxiety around in relation to another pregnancy. 'However much the parents are reassured that it won't happen again, they won't believe you, so I help them find ways to support themselves in that feeling of anxiety rather than battening it down.'

According to Julia, there are other types of early loss which seldom get acknowledged.

Some parents elect to terminate a pregnancy because a severe disability has been diagnosed. This is an enormous decision that the family has to live with for the rest of their lives. To make this decision needs time, proper information and emotional support, which are sometimes in short supply.

On the other hand, parents might choose to keep the baby knowing that it will be born with a disability; or, to take another scenario, the baby might be born with a serious condition that went undiagnosed in the womb. Parents have expectations and dreams for perfect babies. If their babies are born with severe disabilities they are naturally shocked and full of grief. It takes time to come to terms with the new situation. Feelings of grief and disappointment might feel like an indulgence in the face of all the practical complications they are faced with, but it is natural to have them nevertheless.

Family break-up has become a common cause of grief in families. In Britain, about four in ten current marriages will end in divorce. This does not even take into account relationship break-up outside marriage. Rather than analyse the reasons for the rising divorce trend I will concentrate on the emotional effects. Those involved think separation will be a solution to their problems, but few are prepared for the huge emotional and physical impact it causes. They underestimate the complexity and strength of the bonds that have tied them together. Every aspect of their lives from breakfast to bed has been intertwined. Tearing the bonds apart hurts a great deal. It comes as no surprise to me that divorce is considered the worst stressor after bereavement. The major difference is the element of choice. Death is not a chosen option, whereas divorce is sought, at least by one partner, in the hope that a better outcome will ensue. The emotions experienced after a break-up are similar to a bereavement and can affect every family member in three generations. It is sometimes forgotten how deeply grandparents can suffer if their grandchildren are prevented from seeing them.

The adults, and any children who are involved, experience a roller-coaster of emotions. The break-up is likely to have been preceded by years of arguments, bitterness, blaming and anger. If one partner leaves unexpectedly, the other will be left in a state of shock and denial. The most common emotions are sadness, anger and guilt. The confusion and destabilization that follow separation can last from one to three years. The process of reorganization is challenging. The first task to be accomplished is to grieve the lost marriage. Even though so many marriages in Britain break down today, people still enter into them with love, optimism and hope, believing that they will be together 'until death us do part'. It is not surprising if the main participants grieve for the loss of their ideals, hopes and dreams, as do all those around them who supported and celebrated their union.

A separation or divorce usually entails profound practical changes that often mean loss of social status. The family home might have to be sold, smaller accommodation found in another area, and schools changed. This is a time of confusion and destabilization for everyone. Feeling out of control is a common emotion. A second useful task here is try and see what went wrong and to accept some responsibility for it. This makes it possible to draw a line under the past and learn from it.

Gradually, new routines and boundaries are established, and the new lifestyle becomes the norm. The past no longer has to be viewed as negative but can be remembered in its entirety with both good and bad elements. For this to happen, support from the wider family and friends is essential. If they cannot provide what is necessary, mediation and counselling can be helpful. Adults need to find a modus vivendi for the sake of their children as well as for themselves.

In her autobiography, *Memoirs of an Unfit Mother*, Anne

Robinson of *The Weakest Link* fame describes the break-up of her first marriage after the birth of her baby daughter.

Our home was filled with confusion, suspicion and an ever-present feeling of resentment and loss on both sides. Whatever magic had brought her parents together had gone. Her father was disappointed at how his married life had turned out. Her mother was desperate to be freed from a husband whom she saw as a despot.

She goes on to recount how in 1973 she lost custody, care and control of her daughter because of her career and her drink problem, even though her ex-husband, who got custody, also had a career and a drink problem. Having hit rock bottom, she tackled her alcoholism, sorted out her emotional problems and managed to be a parent and have a career. Looking back, she acknowledges that they were young and inexperienced. 'Our only pride is that we emerged on the other side. We are still parents to a bright, loving, funny and beautiful young woman.'

7

More Losses

Redundancy, which is a polite word for getting the sack, can have a big impact on physical and psychological health. I have lost count of the number of men and women who have come to see me with depression following forced redundancy. It is not surprising, considering the way we invest much of our time and energy in our work. Our work provides us with status and self-confidence. To lose it is often to lose a part of ourselves. Peter came to see me after he lost his job. He told me:

> I've always given 150 per cent to my work. Now I feel like a gigantic failure. Financially, and in every way, I seem to have gone back to square one. I was working 16 hours a day and it affected my relationship. At first my girlfriend was supportive but she's fed up and doesn't like to see me so weak. I am confused about what to do with my life now.

After talking more about the process of grief and the time needed to recover from stressful events, Peter was able to accept his negative feelings better. Sorting out the turmoil gave him space to reassess his lifestyle. He realized for the first time that he liked the buzz of extremes but there was a price to pay in mental and physical health.

Joan Christmas, a career coach with years of experience, fully understands the emotional component of job loss.

> Most people who come to see me go through the classic phases of grief. First shock, then anger and outrage. 'How could this happen to me?' It is a rejection and a great loss when you think how it means loss of income, colleagues, routine and a place in society. First I try and stay with the anger and grief for as long as it takes, though sometimes I have to jerk them out of it. Then I work on building up self-confidence and self-esteem by putting them in touch with their skills again. They need to get back a sense of control over events that have spiralled out of their control. I hope they end up having more perspective on their lives. I remind them

that when all is said and done it is just a job, and finding a new job is just a process.

If job loss causes grief, consider the magnitude for someone who loses everything at once – home, family, possessions, job, culture and language. This is what happens to emigrants who are forced to flee their homelands as a result of persecution, war, famine or natural disasters. Migration has always been a feature of world history, and not necessarily a negative one. If people move from one place to another to better their working and living conditions the losses involved are more than balanced out by the gains. The most painful translocations are the involuntary ones. One of the worst examples is the slave trade in the seventeenth and eighteenth centuries when Africans were captured and sent in chains to America and the Caribbean to work as manual labourers, often in terrible conditions. The grief they felt still echoes down to us in the soulful Negro spirituals they sang to express their longing for home.

More recently, the nineteenth century witnessed the migration of hundreds of thousands of Irish to America because of starvation caused by the potato famine. A huge influx of Jewish immigrants forced by pogroms out of Eastern Europe and Russia arrived in Britain at the turn of the twentieth century. Another influx of Jews from Germany and Austria arrived around the outbreak of World War II. Today, war, famine and tyrannical regimes in certain areas of the world continue to ensure a steady flow of asylum seekers to Europe.

The grief process for asylum seekers is complicated by several factors. One is the scale of their loss. They leave behind them all the things that gave them a sense of identity – their families, their status, their livelihoods, culture and achievements. They must start from scratch, relying only on inner resources for their sense of identity. Second, the shock of the upheaval and of the traumatic events preceding it means that they may well be experiencing all the physical and mental symptoms of post-traumatic stress disorder. Third, they cannot move back and forth from loss-orientation to restoration-orientation because of the enormity of the dislocation they are experiencing. Their grief might have to be denied or put on hold while they grapple with the overwhelming practical challenges of their new situations. They need to learn English, find lawyers, get housed and find a job. Their energies have to be focused on the fight for survival rather than feelings of loss. Grieving is a luxury.

In his prize-winning book *The Emigrants*, the German academic and writer W. G. Sebald (who incidentally settled in England) reconstructs the lives of four Jews who were forced into exile around the outbreak of World War II. He describes how they rebuilt their lives, created new relationships and became successful in their chosen professions. The reader is seduced into thinking how well they have adjusted until we learn how in their old age they are overwhelmed by feelings of postponed grief. *The Kite Runner* by Khaled Hosseini describes the grief of an old Afghan refugee in America through the eyes of his more adaptable son.

> He missed the sugarcane fields of Jalalabad and the gardens of Paghman. He missed people milling in and out of his house, missed walking down the bustling aisles of Shor Bazaar and greeting people who knew him and his father, knew his grandfather, people who shared ancestors with him, whose pasts inter-twined with his.
>
> Khaled Hosseini, *The Kite Runner*

Through the services of a counsellor I had a very moving interview with Mina, a handsome Iranian woman in her mid-forties. In danger for her life, she fled to Britain in 2001 where she is still seeking asylum. For nearly four years she has been struggling for survival in a quagmire of bureaucratic and legal obstacles. She has no permanent lodging, no money and is forbidden to work until her legal status is clarified. Mina was persecuted by the repressive Islamic regime in Iran because she is Kurdish, non-Muslim and an activist for women's rights. First she was thrown out of her teaching post and then she was thrown into prison, where she was tortured and raped. Eventually, when pamphlets and writings which were considered subversive were discovered in her home, she was forced to flee Iran, leaving her husband and children behind.

> Like my Kurdish grandfather I have always been a fighter and fought so hard for the cause of women. I used to bear persecution because I believed that one day I would be free to pass on what I had learnt and continue my work for the advancement of women.

The Paradise of freedom beckoned. But coming to Britain where I am not wanted has broken me into a thousand pieces. I have lost my identity. I no longer remember the person I was. I feel powerless. I feel worse than nothing. In Iran I was proud of my activities even though I knew they would affect my family. Here I have lost hope.

My worst sorrow is having to leave my children. I don't miss having to take orders from other people. I don't miss the way I was treated as a woman. It would make me happy to know that Islamic women could be independent like women in Britain. At times I have felt so low I wonder that I have survived. From a young age I learnt from my grandfather that if you know a lot you will have responsibilities that will bear down on you. When I came out of prison he told me that I had to be strong, stronger than iron which is hardened in the fire. He taught me that life is not just about survival but about bettering one's condition. Right now I feel much more angry than sad. In my prison in Iran I had a cause I believed in. The torture and hunger I suffered are nothing in comparison to the grief I am suffering in this the biggest and hardest prison I have been in.

I hope that Mina's sad story will have a happy ending. As history shows, the majority of immigrants to this country have not only survived but thrived, despite racism, prejudice and disadvantages. The first generation might not always have become fully integrated socially themselves but the likelihood is that their children will do so. They have given the rest of us shining examples of how to deal courageously and positively with loss and grief.

Grief is usually a temporary condition. People experience it, process it and move on. But for those who live with a serious chronic mental or physical disease like bipolar disorder, multiple sclerosis or motor neurone disease, to name but a few, grief is an on-going condition in relation to the continuous losses caused by the disease.

Charlotte Johnson Wahl, who is a distinguished artist, vividly describes the relentless war of attrition that she has to fight against Parkinson's disease.

When I was first given the diagnosis 16 years ago the shock was horrendous. I couldn't take it in all at once. It took at least a year

51

to get over it. The news was delivered by a foolish neurologist whom I no longer see. He told me above all not to read or talk about Parkinson's to anybody. I did what he advised for about three months while the anxiety grew and grew. Then I decided to ignore him, and I read everything about the disease that I could lay my hands on and felt the better for it. The sense of loss is instantaneous and part of the shock. What you lose is that sense of happy confidence of which you have not really been conscious. Although we all know we are going to get old and die one day, there's something unpleasant about knowing that you are facing an uncertain length of time in which you are going to lose your ability to move. I do get angry and start shouting to myself. And if I am sad and crying about something else then Parkinson's comes in like a chorus of grief. It is always there in the wings, waiting, and makes me howl like a dog.

At first the effects of the Parkinson's were not so noticeable. But now it is difficult to control my movements. I can tip to the right and knock people over in shops. My body is stiff and I can fall without warning. I get constant infections and have to spend hours in bed. Now I have started to choke on my food, which is really frightening. But the worst for me is fatigue, sheer fatigue. My backbone melts, I can't talk or swallow. I don't even have the strength to answer the telephone.

One of the hardest things is looking odd and becoming odd. Strangers think I am drunk or mad. They stare at me in restaurants and in the streets. I don't blame them – they are not wicked, just frightened. It frightens me to see photos now because I can see the development of the Parkinsonian face that has a fixed and angry look because the muscles are not working. I mind so much that I used to dance so well and was the captain of gym at school and was always fit and quick moving. And when people used to stare at me it was because I was attractive. One's vanity takes a terrible knock. It's offended by falling and being stiff and walking in a strange way. I envy my friends who are pretty. I envy their energy. I worry about not being able to look after my friends. I fear that they might abandon me. Like an army on the march. If you can't keep up you will get left behind. I dread seeing people after a long interval lest they are saying to themselves, 'Is this really the Charlotte I once knew?'

How do I cope? The surprising thing is that despite all I've said, I am optimistic about my future. I don't feel doomed. I refuse to give up. I have come to terms with the fact that I am likely to die young. It seems faintly ludicrous to pretty oneself up and it is difficult to put on eye make-up, and yet I feel one should try and make the effort. I do try to be gentle with myself when I don't get round to doing my tax returns, or can't finish a painting, or neglect my friends. My children, grandchildren and friends keep me going. I don't allow myself to dwell on the negative things that I have described to you. I don't often say, 'Why me?' I don't plan for the future, or try to work out what it's going to be. I think my strange optimism comes from going from day to day.

'Disenfranchised grief' is a term used by experts to describe grief that is difficult for someone to openly express in society, and for society to recognize as legitimate. People with HIV or AIDS can experience such grief. Human Immunodeficiency Virus attacks the body's immune system, leaving it open to serious infections. There is no cure or vaccine for HIV, which develops into AIDS and kills millions of people every year in Africa and other parts of the world. In Britain, however, where sophisticated medication is available on the NHS, the virus can now be controlled by a cocktail of anti-retroviral drugs so that the number of deaths has dramatically fallen from its peak in 1995. Nevertheless, those who become infected with the virus do have to adapt to living with a life-threatening disease that people associate with the stigma of sexual transmission. The extra elements involved in disenfranchised grief were explained to me by a psychotherapist who works with individuals, gay couples and family members affected by HIV/AIDS.

The people who come and see me are not always aware they are going through a grief process. They can't name it. It just feels like a turmoil of emotions. They are on such a roller-coaster they feel as if they are going mad. The solid ground they were walking on has just been split by an earthquake. The old reference points have disappeared and with them the old thought processes. The shock is enormous, even if they have volunteered for the test. And there is denial, of course. People initially often talk about other problems like housing or relationships rather than HIV itself.

Then there is fear. They immediately think they are going to die. Sadness and depression sets in with the realization that they are no longer the fit and healthy people they once were. They feel that their freedom has been taken away. A lot of people get stuck in the depressive stage. I liken this to an injured animal needing to go into its cave to lick its wounds. Guilt can be a heavy burden. They might feel they have brought this on themselves, or passed it on to someone else. They worry about whether to tell their loved ones. Anger is tricky. I think it is very healthy to feel angry if it doesn't come out in negative behaviour. But with HIV anger can be held down by shame. Or it can't be openly acknowledged, because how can they express anger about something that is secret?

The taboo around sexual disease poses the greatest problem for these people. They might feel contaminated, or be viewed as contaminated by others who chastise and judge them through fear and ignorance. This can be very isolating. If a gay partner does die of AIDS, grief can be compounded if the surviving partner is excluded by the family from the funeral. When people are diagnosed with HIV they fear they won't be able to make new relationships, especially sexual ones. They can, of course, but it will be harder . . . they have to make real changes in their lives to help themselves stay healthy. Families go through grief too. Parents ask themselves where they went wrong, or what they could have done differently. They have to live with the worry of death too.

There are positive things to do to help. The first is to get proper information for themselves and those close to them. The Terrence Higgins Trust has courses and provides practical information that lowers anxiety immediately. They need to work on leading healthy lives because the immune system needs boosting for the drugs to be effective. They must eat well, take exercise and find people to talk to. Counselling can provide a safe, non-judgemental environment for them to process their grief. I feel I can be a witness, sometimes the only witness, to this. I know they are moving on when they have come out of the cave, make new social connections and make new decisions for their future lives in the context of a healthier lifestyle. I am constantly impressed by the strength people find to cope.

One of the most interesting cases I was involved with concerned a 16-year-old boy who lost his belief that the world was a secure and safe place. He was standing on the platform in a London Underground station when the man beside him hurled himself in front of an incoming train. When Philip came for therapy he was, not surprisingly, feeling traumatized. He was experiencing panic attacks and flashbacks, and was finding it difficult to eat and sleep. His physical symptoms receded gradually. It was the shock to his belief system that was more challenged. In retrospect he recollected a lot of detail about the victim's clothes and features 'which looked so very ordinary'. The violent act he witnessed was so unexpected and arbitrary that it shook his world. Having had a happy, stable and prosperous childhood he had grown up with an optimistic and positive view of life. Now he felt vulnerable. The world no longer seemed a safe place. He found himself picking up on frightening and violent stories in the media that he had never noticed before. And he could not bring himself to travel underground. After a few months in the company of some school friends he got himself back in the train, but although he was able to look at this as a gain in experience as well as a loss of innocence, his sense of security about the world was not restored.

Some people who seek therapy feel robbed of a normal childhood. Ideally children have the right to be protected and cared for by adults so that they can enjoy home and school life in as carefree a way as possible. They can be spontaneous, happy, creative and funny within a safe and secure environment. One woman with whom I worked was finding it difficult to make close relationships. As her story unfolded she experienced a flood of pent-up grief for what amounted to a lost childhood. For five years of her young life she had been sexually abused by her mother's boyfriend, who was supposed to be looking after her while her mother went out to work.

A lost childhood is hard to retrieve but I do believe that this wonderful woman healed some of her wounds. She was able to tell her mother what had happened and her mother had listened and believed. Working with me, she began to realize that what had happened to her was not her fault and that in many secret ways she had resisted the advances of this man. She felt that the angry feelings that she had repressed for so long were justified. She began to hope that she might be able to trust herself in an adult relationship. And she knew with certainty that if she ever had children of her own she would make sure that they were nurtured and protected.

8

Children and grief

The first loss a child is likely to experience in the natural course of events is the death of a grandparent. Grandparents can be significant and beloved figures in the lives of their grandchildren, especially if they have been involved in day-to-day care. Children can feel their loss keenly, and will be aware of the sadness of their parents too. I have been to funerals where children as young as six or seven have participated by handing out service sheets, showing people to their seats or even speaking some words. Children need mourning rituals as much as adults. I wish I had been given such an opportunity when I was a child.

Another early loss could be the death of a pet. Michael Gordon, a London vet who has been practising for over 30 years, believes that children can learn about a good death if they are involved when a dog or cat is put down.

I provide a private room for the family. I give a sedative first so when the last injection is administered to the animal there is no crying, discomfort or protest. This can also be done at home if the family prefers it. I give them the option of having the ashes back so that they can be strewn or kept in a box. They can have the body and bury it in the garden, but must dig deep because of hygiene and foxes. I know lots of families who have created burial rituals for themselves. Young children can be upset but are tougher than their parents believe. The ones who are grief-stricken are adolescents. If you think of it, they may have known the animal all their lives and been involved in their care. They really can deeply feel the loss of their companion and loyal friend.

Over 150,000 children a year in Britain are affected by family break-up. These children have to cope with enormous emotional and physical challenges. This description by Tom, who is 15, is not untypical.

I live with my mum in the week and go to my dad's house at weekends. He got married again to a woman who had been a friend of the family. She has a son a year older than me and her son is living in the same house. It was hard to get by at first. When I went to one house from the other there were, like, different sets of rules, and it was hard to adapt to. I used to get into fights with the other kid.

Belinda's idea of an ideal family was shattered.

Moving really upset me because then I knew we would never be able to do things as a family again. I'm the sort of person who likes things to stay the same. I felt quite isolated in the flat we moved to. I couldn't see my friends and my dad was living quite far away. Now it's settled down to having Sunday with him. There was a friend of mine whose parents had split up and she couldn't see her dad because he was living in another country. And there was another girl who didn't even know her dad. And I felt lucky.

How can separating parents best help their grieving and disorientated children? First, they can be clear about the reality of what is going on. Children need to know exactly what is going to happen to them when their home breaks up, otherwise they fantasize about being abandoned or rejected. Parents need to reorganize themselves as quickly as possible so that their children can get back to leading a normal life. This might involve freeing them from caring for an adult or siblings. Parents need to be able to listen and stay with their children's sadness and anger for as long as it takes. This is much easier said than done, because parents feel guilty about hurting their children and want to believe that they are fine. Children need permission to express the anger they feel because it is frightening feeling this way with the adults they love.

Parents need to absolve their children of any sense of guilt for the break-up. It is surprising how often children fear that their behaviour caused problems between their parents, and might need a great deal of reassurance that this was not so. Parents need to make a superhuman effort not to use the children as pawns in their own conflict. There is a difference between a painful divorce and a damaging one. Using the children as weapons makes for a damaging divorce. And lastly, adults need to know that the adjustment and recovery process can take years. A break-up is not a single event. Children are required to adapt to many profound changes that flow from it. As well as adjusting to new homes, new routines and to new social and economic conditions, they probably have to adjust to their parents' new partners. Some 2.5 million of them end up living in stepfamilies, coping with sets of new relationships that are emotionally challenging. It is worth pointing out that these children, however well they appear to have adjusted, might experience surprisingly powerful feelings of loss and anxiety as adults when they are faced with changes or endings.

The death of a parent, primary carer or sibling is the most severe loss a child can experience. I have emphasized the need to respect individual ways of grieving and mourning, but advice from experts can be reassuring for adults who are involved with bereaved children. They can also get support from the growing number of excellent child bereavement organizations that I list at the end. I shall again be drawing on the experience of William Worden, who believes that children need to go though the same grieving tasks as adults. He lists the particular needs of bereaved children as follows: they need adequate information about the death; their fears and anxieties need to be addressed; they need reassurance that they are not to blame; they need to be heard; their feelings need validation; they need to be involved and included in the mourning rituals, and at the same time their routine activities need to continue; they need opportunities to remember.

Children manifest their feelings in very varied and different ways. They may deny feelings out of shock or disbelief. They may act out their distress rather than expressing it in words. They may be sad and anxious or they may not show much emotion at all. Young children may cry in an uninhibited way, while teenagers may prefer to cry in isolation. They can feel very angry at being abandoned. Feelings of helplessness, injustice and frustration get rolled into fury. Guilt can be a burden for children of all ages.

Before they can rationalize properly young children might get it into their heads that their noisiness or naughtiness killed their parent. Adolescents who are generally in conflict with parents in their bid for more independence may feel dreadful because they had been argumentative, rude or defiant before the death of the parent. It is too late to say sorry and too late to say, 'I love you.' One adolescent who shouted at his father that he wished he was dead after being grounded for a minor offence was traumatized when his father died of a heart attack the following day. Children often manifest their grief through physical symptoms, either real or imaginary. They might complain of headaches, feeling sick or aches and pains. These might serve as excuses not to go to school. Worden discovered that bereaved children, especially boys, suffer more accidents, like broken limbs, than usual. This could be because their concentration is affected or because subconsciously they are taking more risks.

Children very naturally feel a high level of anxiety when a parent or carer dies. The disappearance of such an important person in their lives shakes their whole world. If they lose one person, why not another? Below the age of six the bereaved child tends to become clingy. 'When her father died of cancer Emily wouldn't let me out of her sight,' explained Deborah. 'She slept in my bed with all her soft toys around her. She started to suck her thumb again. She wouldn't go to nursery school for weeks and weeks.' Children of all ages quickly pick up if the surviving parent is not coping and become even more anxious. Adolescents can be well aware if there are financial difficulties and worry about money. They worry for themselves and their surviving parent. They might get even more frightened by experiencing panic attacks.

The death of a parent in the child-rearing years is not a natural event. It is usually the result of a terminal illness or an accident. Of the three of my friends who died in their early forties, one was drowned, another had a sudden brain haemorrhage while jogging, and another was killed in a car accident. When untimely death happens like this, concerned adults are in a state of shock and misery themselves. The first and natural instinct is probably to protect the children from the same pain they are suffering. They might decide to send the children off to stay with friends or relatives. The funeral service might be held without them.The children might be observed playing happily with friends as if nothing had happened and it is supposed that they are not grieving.

At this point it would be more helpful for adults to behave counter-intuitively and not protect them from grief. A child bereavement counsellor I interviewed put it this way:

My job is just to get people talking. Adults are frightened of talking to children. They think they might do more harm than good. But children are so good, resilient and forgiving that saying something is so much better than saying nothing. Rather than asking how they are feeling, try asking them to tell the story of what happened and what is happening now. It is easier for children to explain this way. These conversations need to be on-going over time because bereaved youngsters will feel the loss the most during important transitions in their lives. For instance, when moving from primary to secondary school, or going to university, or even when getting married.

Worden believes that, taking into account the cognitive ability of different ages, children need to go through the same grieving tasks as adults. First, they need to accept the reality of the loss. To do this they need to be told, accurately and in language they can understand, that their grandparent, mother, father, brother or sister has died and will not be coming back. Explaining is not as easy as it sounds because the adults involved may not have articulated their own beliefs about death even to themselves. Explaining about the physical side of death is more straightforward, especially if children have already experienced the death of a pet. Explaining what happens afterwards can be more challenging. Such explanations will depend on different religious and cultural beliefs. Some children for instance, can get confused about Heaven and Hell. They might find the notion that someone lives on in spirit and can be 'talked to' deeply comforting, or they might get confused about ghosts.

If someone dies suddenly and away from home a child needs to be told how that person died. Children have incredible imaginations and will fantasize if they are not told the truth. When my son was five, he had a curious conversation with my mother (his grandmother) about death. She told him she was shrinking as she got older. When my son started to have bad dreams and I got to the bottom of his anxiety, it transpired that he was haunted by the image of his beloved granny ending up in a matchbox. Between us we were able to set the record straight for him. The death of his granny some years later was the first significant loss in his life and I very much regret that I did not take him to her funeral.

If children are not told an accurate version of the truth, they might learn it from people who are not well meaning. A secret is very hard to keep even if people are well meaning. The worst case I heard was of a seven-year-old boy who told his school friends that his father had died of a heart attack. He even felt quite proud saying this because it made him different from the others. 'That's not what I heard,' quipped one of the boys. 'My mum said he committed suicide and blew his brains out with a shotgun. They went splatter, splatter, splatter all over the ground.' Naturally this boy was traumatized. He did not even know what suicide meant and has had a problem trusting his mother ever since. A suicide is a very hard thing to explain to young children but there are simple and truthful ways of explaining that a parent was ill, overworked, crushed by worries and couldn't cope any longer. Advice can be obtained from counsellors, local bereavement services and the excellent books listed at the end of this book.

As a child I was not taken to a single funeral. Today, experts recommend that even very young children are included in funeral ceremonies, provided enough support can be offered to the bereaved adults so that they can focus on their own grief rather than worrying about their child. Worden even suggests that young children could be given the choice of whether they would like to view the body in the funeral home, which is a more common practice in America than in Britain. They should, however, be well prepared by being told in detail what to expect. Young children need very careful explanations about burials or cremations. It is hard for them to conceive of a body being buried or burnt without it hurting. Children can feel very angry at being left out or ignored when someone dies. Involving them in the funeral arrangements gives them a participating role. They can choose hymns and prayers if there is a service. They can make or choose precious objects or draw pictures that can be placed in the coffin. I heard recently of three young children under 12 who painted every surface of a plain wooden coffin for their mother. It took a few days and was a comforting way to express their grief in a practical way. Being given a place in the funeral procession or a task such as throwing earth or a flower on to the coffin at a burial can be important rituals for a child. I have heard children as young as seven recite poems at a funeral service.

Someone recently told me of a sensitive alternative they thought had worked for their grandchildren of three and five. A few days after the burial, when the grave was covered with flowers, the pastor arranged a small service for the children with just a few members of the immediate family. He spoke in words the children understood and they laid bunches of flowers with drawings on the grave. A young child could be involved in the planting of a memorial tree, which they help water and watch grow over many years. Involvement at this level and in this detail helps children of all ages to accept the reality of the death of their mother or father.

Worden's second task for children is to help them experience the pain and intense emotions. Adults' natural reaction is to protect children from the sight and sound of their own sorrow. It is in fact more helpful for adults to share their emotions with the children. The way children deal with their emotions can be disconcerting. They cannot tolerate as much pain as adults so theirs is expressed in brief bursts. They might be sitting crying in a corner one minute and then tearing round the garden with the dog the next. Adolescents often want to get out of the house to be with friends, doing normal things. These shifting moods should not be prematurely read as children having got over their grief. It is so important for the surviving adult to be able to listen to their children's worries, talk to them and mourn with them.

This degree of availability may just be too much for the grief-stricken surviving parent. A widow I know whose husband died suddenly when she was 40 was left in such financial straits that she had to start a job almost immediately. Her two daughters did not blame the father for dying but held a lifelong grudge against the mother for being emotionally unavailable to them, which was never resolved. Men often deal with their grief by throwing themselves into work which cuts them off from their children. All too often what happens is the building of a wall of silence. After a while the dead mother or father stops being talked about. Children understand that this is what the parent wants, and the parent thinks that silence on the part of children means they have recovered.

The third task for children is to adjust to a life in which the dead person is missing. This takes time. When a principal carer or sibling dies the dynamics of the family change profoundly. Practical circumstances may also change radically. The bereaved parent might even have to leave the family home and move back to his or her parents or to another geographical area, leading to huge changes for everyone. At this point much will depend on the parenting functions of the surviving parent, who in effect becomes a single parent with a dual role. This might mean giving up work, or working in a different job. It might mean learning to cook, clean and shop. It might mean becoming more involved with the children. Losing a mother usually leads to more changes in routine. Losing a father can make discipline and organization in the home more of a struggle. Grandparents often become actively involved in child rearing again at a time when they were enjoying retirement. All these changes feel overwhelming at first. Although it is not always possible, families cope better if the children can stay in the same home and at the same school, if economic circumstances are not affected, and if there is practical and emotional support from family and friends. If the same rules and routine can be maintained as far as possible, children will feel more secure. If there are a lot of disruptions, chaos and lack of support, then families might not cope so well. Bereaved children will have fewer problems if the surviving parent maintains consistent discipline.

Children can find themselves catapulted into new roles too. The oldest child often feels burdened with responsibilities for the surviving parent or younger brothers and sisters. In larger families the oldest daughter sometimes takes on the mothering role for the younger ones. One of the classic mistakes which is often made by well-meaning adults is to tell a boy that he is now the man of the house and must help his mother, or vice versa with a girl. Children take up responsibility only too quickly without being given an injunction to do so.

A death of a sibling can be really hard on the rest of the children. Frequently when a child dies young it is after a long terminal illness. During this time it is inevitable that the time and attention of the parents are focused on the sick child. This can lead to jealousy, loneliness or a feeling of not being equally loved. Brothers and sisters need as much space for talking about their loss as do the grieving parents.

A heart-rending account of sibling death concerns J. M. Barrie, the author of *Peter Pan*. Barrie was six when his older brother David was killed in a skating accident. His mother's grief for her favourite child was catastrophic. In *Margaret Ogilvy*, a portrait of his mother which he wrote years later, Barrie recounted how he crept into the darkened room where she was lying with her face turned to the wall. When she heard him enter the room his mother spoke to him.

> I think the tone hurt me, for I made no answer, and then the voice said more anxiously, 'Is that you?' again. I thought it was the dead boy she was speaking to, and I said in a little lonely voice, 'No, it's no' him, it's just me.' After that I sat a great deal in her bed trying to make her forget him.

The sensitive little boy taught himself to whistle and swagger like his dead brother and dressed up in his clothes, but to no avail. 'She lived twenty-nine years after his death . . . But I had not made her forget the bit of her that was dead, in those nine-and-twenty years he was not removed one day farther from her.'

Worden's fourth task is to emotionally relocate the dead parent in the child's life. In her book *Death Talk*, family therapist Glenda Fredman talks of 'co-memorating'. Gathering people together to share living memories about someone has a different feel to it than mourning the death of someone. With the help of adults, children can do this on an on-going basis. Ordinary things, like keeping photos on display, remembering anniversaries, hearing stories from grandparents and friends, have a greater healing effect than expunging memories altogether. The grandmother of the two little boys who had the private funeral service is remembering and writing down in albums all the stories about their father she thinks will interest them as they grow up. Not only is this a comfort to her but it will enable the boys to have a continuing internal dialogue with their father when they feel sad about things, or win prizes at school or in their dreams. Children need to remember and carry on with their lives at the same time.

When should adults start worrying about a grieving child? If after a reasonable amount of time a child continues to have physical ailments, refuses to talk, is acting out with bad behaviour, getting into trouble at school, is depressed or is developing an eating disorder, then professional advice should be sought from local bereavement services. For very young children play therapy is often used. Individual sessions with an outsider can be supportive for older children who do not have an appropriate adult in whom to confide. Counsellors who have worked in hospice settings with families before and after the death of a parent know how helpful such conversations can be. It can be very comforting for the dying person too to be able to talk about the small and big things that are important now and would have been important in the future. Schools can be a great escape and resource for some children and teachers can help both parents and children by giving them an opportunity to talk. They can also make sure there is no bullying when the child is particularly vulnerable.

In a nutshell: children cannot be protected from grief. All children and adolescents grieve even though they express it differently from adults. Grieving is a long-term process during which they will revisit their grief, and in their minds and conversation construct a changing relationship with the person who has died. Younger children will need help in retaining good memories. They will be influenced by and take their cues from the way in which the significant adults around them grieve.

9

Severe grief

The death of a child and death by suicide are considered to be among the severest forms of bereavement. This is because there are extra dimensions involved. To outlive a child that we have created is to violate a law of nature. As parents we are programmed to bond with and protect our babies. Parents continue to feel protective towards their children even when they are grown up and no longer helpless. Today, in our western societies the majority of us expect our children to outlive us, not the other way round. Even in previous centuries, when infant mortality was much higher, parents who lost children were not inured to grief. There is a beautiful story of the Prophet Muhammad, who founded the religion of Islam in the seventh century, showing him as a tender and sorrowing father. Five of his six children had already died when a son was born to him by Maria, the Egyptian. Muhammad was overjoyed and was often to be seen carrying the baby through the city. When the child fell mortally ill at the age of two, people started gathering at the house. When a follower asked whether he wept, the Prophet replied, 'These tears are a mercy. The eye weeps and the heart grieves and we say nothing but what pleases our Lord. Ah Ibrahim, how grieved we are by your departure!' In 1899, Josephine, the firstborn and much beloved daughter of the writer Rudyard Kipling, died at the age of seven. Years later in a letter to a father who had also lost a son, Kipling wrote, 'People say that kind of wound heals. It doesn't. It only skins over.'

The death of a child will always have a profound effect on the dynamics of the family. Parents may not be able to give each other emotional or moral support at such a time. The child is likely to have had a long terminal illness that is very stressful, or to have died in an accident which is very shocking. Father might be anxious to put the tragedy behind and get on with living, while Mother is still too sad and depressed to have hope for the future. Parents will have had dreams, hopes and expectations for their child. To have those dashed is hard. Parents suffer from guilt – in a general way for not having been able to protect their child, more specifically if they have been

67

unable to prevent suffering. They may end up blaming each other too. It is quite common for parents to separate after losing a child, thus compounding the loss and misery.

Neither parent might have the resources to comfort and support any other child who will be feeling as shocked and bereft as they are, as well as feeling neglected and left out. Surviving children might experience their parents, out of anxiety or guilt, behaving differently towards them. I know a family whose child was drowned in a swimming pool while on holiday. It was a tragic accident but the parents became over-protective with the two remaining children, whose independence and freedom were curtailed. Sometimes, parents invest too many emotions and expectations in a new baby.

A piece of advice which Jenny, whose son died in a plane crash, wanted to pass on was the importance of being able to say goodbye.

> I will never forgive myself for not going to the funeral home to see his body. Everyone told me not to but I should have followed my own instincts. I needed to hold his hand. A mother needs to touch her son. I didn't say goodbye.

She still finds it difficult when anyone asks her how many children she has. If she mentions two without adding her dead son she feels bad. If she does include him, the conversation can become embarrassing or tortuous.

Bereaved people fear that in letting go of grief they might be denying the significance of the loved one. Shakespeare, in his inimitable way, found the perfect words to express this dilemma in *King John*.

> Grief fills the room up of my absent child,
> Lies in his bed, walks up and down with me.
> Puts on his pretty looks, repeats his words,
> Remembers me of all his gracious parts,
> Stuffs out his vacant garments with his form:
> Then have I reason to be fond of grief.

Rabbi Harold Kushner deals with this problem in his best-selling book, *When Bad Things Happen to Good People*. Kushner wrote this book after his child died of an incurable congenital disease. He believes that life would be dangerous, perhaps unliveable, if we could not feel pain. This does not mean he meekly accepted his son's death. On the contrary, he raged at the unfairness of the tragedy that hit his whole family. But in time he was able to rise beyond the question, 'Why did it happen?' to ask, 'What do I do now that it has happened?' He learnt that he could let go of grief without letting go of the love he had for his son.

The donation of organs may not be possible, or religiously or socially acceptable to some people, but parents who agree to donate appear to gain great comfort from the knowledge that the life they lost has helped others to live. As many as five different people can be helped by receiving different organs. Transplant co-ordinators in hospitals can facilitate communication channels for donor families and recipients if that is wanted. Recipients are able to send letters and photos, expressing their gratitude to the families. Meetings can be arranged too. I read of a man of 65 who had a liver transplanted from a boy of 18. The boy's family wanted to meet him. They all became firm friends and the family acquired a proxy grandfather.

It may be invidious to measure grief, but I do believe that death by suicide is the hardest of all losses to bear. First, it tends to be both unexpected and violent. In addition, it gets dragged into the legal and public domain. It is highly emotionally charged and has awkward social implications. If we have not been directly affected by suicide ourselves, most of us know families that have. Every year in Britain 100,000 people find themselves in hospital as a result of deliberate self-poisoning or injury. Attempted suicides and suicides of young people are frequently linked to alcohol and drug abuse. Young people who have suffered sexual or physical abuse are also at increased risk. Within the prison population young prisoners represent the largest group of individuals at risk of killing themselves. Suicide among the old is strongly associated with depression, illness and loneliness.

A suicide is invariably a terrible shock. It appears to come out of the blue. Even individuals who have made previous attempts or had a long depressive illness often commit suicide at a point when they appear to be getting better. The shock of the unexpected is exacerbated by the physical violence involved. Suicide victims frequently kill themselves by shooting, hanging, poisoning, suffocating, drowning or falling from bridges. The bereaved find it extremely difficult and painful having to deal with this aspect of death.

In her excellent book, *A Special Scar*, Alison Wertheimer explains some of the difficulties around the language of suicide. The words are loaded with negative or shameful connotations. Victim, survivor, killed by his own hand, self-inflicted death, unnatural death. None of these terms sound right. Maggie puts it this way. 'Saying my son killed himself or took his life or committed suicide is so much harder than saying my son died or was killed in an accident.' Nancy, whose husband hanged himself, agrees. 'Eight years on and I just cannot bring myself to say these words. When I tell people that my husband died, I anticipate with dread further questions that might follow.'

It is important to bereaved families to be allowed to mourn in private. Indeed, high-profile personalities frequently make a public appeal for the right to do this. The family of a suicide victim automatically loses its right to privacy because the police, and subsequently the media, are involved from the start. The task of the police officers who arrive at the scene is to gather enough evidence to rule out foul play. However sympathetic they may be, the factual questions they ask of family members who are reeling with shock can be highly stressful, as Maggie recollects.

> I can't even remember what they looked like or what they said, only that there was a man and a woman. Our son killed himself in the garage by flooding our car with carbon monoxide. But what really upset me was that they took away the note he had written. I had read it but was too shocked to take it in. I think it was mostly a list of bequests but it was the last thing we had of him and it was in his own handwriting. When we asked for it back after the coroner's inquest, it turned out to be lost, which the police admitted only after numerous phone calls. His last words were intended for us and should have remained with us.

On the other hand Nancy had nothing but good words to say about the police. She found them both sensitive and helpful.

Wertheimer interviewed 50 'survivors', which is the term she uses for those who lose loved ones through suicide. Many of these were advised at the time by police, undertakers or well-meaning friends not to go to the funeral home to view the body. Like Jenny, they deeply regretted not having done so. Even if the body had been damaged they felt afterwards that they were deprived of something precious. One of the worst sorrows for survivors is that they have not had a chance to say goodbye. Instead they are left to imagine how the person died. Was there pain and suffering? Was death by drowning or hanging or shooting instantaneous? Thoughts like these can be torture. Being with the body even for a short time can serve as a last farewell. It is not always made clear to relatives that they can have access to photos of the body which are stored in the coroner's records later on if they wish. Professionals and friends should be less hasty with their advice and the bereaved might do well to follow their own instincts. Nancy feels strongly about this. She was able to stay alone with her husband's body in the hospital to which he was taken. Later she and her two children spent time with him in the funeral home. She felt this was important for them all, shocked though they were.

The inquest which inevitably follows suicide is another bureaucratic hurdle to be surmounted. With all its legal paraphernalia, the coroner's court can be extremely intimidating to vulnerable family members, who can feel that they are being grilled, blamed or judged. Although members of the public are not allowed into the courtroom, members of the press are. Suicide is considered worthy of a story in the local press, and for anyone well known it gets headlines in the national newspapers. The coroner will have retained any letters left by the victim. By the time they have been handled and perused by strangers they can feel polluted to the family, who are given copies to retain if they are lucky. Surely it would be possible to do this the other way around.

During the inquest, painful details about the death may be revealed to the family for the first time, which can be traumatic. Nancy was not prepared for the medical officer's report. 'It was very shocking to hear the physical details of the post-mortem and to be graphically reminded of the autopsy.' If it is unclear whether death was intended and self-inflicted then the coroner gives an open verdict. This can be helpful to some families, but to others it just leaves a cloud of uncertainty.

The funeral, which can be such a healing ritual in ordinary circumstances, is often fraught with ambiguity. Until very recently attempted suicide was considered a criminal offence in Britain and those who died by suicide could be refused a Christian burial. It was as late as 1961, when the Suicide Act ended prosecutions of those who attempted to kill themselves, that most churches allowed proper burial. But a sense of shame and stigma is still pervasive. Even pastors who take the service can betray their unease. When I went to the funeral of a son of an old friend I was struck by the way the Catholic priest managed to get through the entire service without once mentioning the tragic way he had taken his own life. The church was packed with his friends and work colleagues who were feeling devastated and guilty about his death. It was not until one of them broke down during a reading with the words, 'Oh why, why did you leave us?' that the floodgates were opened and the congregation was able to vent its sorrow. It was only at this point that the funeral service felt authentic.

Because of the stigma, shame and guilt involved, suicide is a delicate subject to discuss. Survivors have been on the receiving end of all kinds of insensitive remarks, like 'Why did she do this to you?' or 'What a waste of a life.' Generally, people are just too embarrassed to say anything appropriate at all. Survivors find themselves in an ambivalent position. If they keep silent it can feel like a denial that their loved one existed; on the other hand, if they tell the truth they may get hurt by negative remarks at a time when they are highly sensitive anyway. 'My sensitivity was so heightened,' Nancy told me, 'that I felt skinned and exposed. My heart felt exposed. The least small thing made me cry or jump even though I was astonished at the level of sympathy and kindness that was shown to me.'

I have worked with several young adults who have entered therapy to talk about the suicide of a parent. They may have been at the point of making a permanent relationship, contemplating having children, or beset by fears that suicide runs in families. They worried that depression or mental instability might be in their genes. What all these cases had in common was suppressed grief. Maybe there had been explanations and conversations in the beginning, but they had faded from memory in the silence that grew up around the suicide. Adults protect children by not talking about the dead parent. Children protect parents from questions that they learn will produce distress. And so gradually a silent taboo is created which no one dares to break.

After the funeral, the survivors are left to try and make sense of a terrible loss that at one level does not make any sense at all. Many suicide victims have had a history of mental disorder and may even have made attempts before. In this instance, the death will not come as a shock and may even bring some relief. But for others, the suicide may come out of the blue. The 'what-ifs', 'whys' and 'if onlys' so common after any death can become a litany of desperation in unexpected suicide. Why did I not pick up the signs? If only I had asked the right questions. I didn't realize the break-up of the relationship had such an impact. Why did he not turn to us for help? She was crying that morning and I had to rush off. Why did no one at the office tell us she was suffering from stress? Such dialogue goes on and on. Relatives try to piece the information together to find a coherent story. Maggie had spoken to her son on the phone a week earlier and had been pleased that things seemed to be going well at work and with the girlfriend. 'If he had died in a car crash we would have comforted ourselves with the thought that he'd died happy. Instead we had to acknowledge that he wasn't happy, was probably severely depressed, and we hadn't known about it.'

The burden of guilt can be very heavy with suicide. It is natural for relatives and friends to berate themselves for failing to stop it. Maybe as a baby there wasn't enough attention. If only we hadn't had so many arguments. Perhaps there was bullying at school and we didn't pick up on it. Survivors are haunted by self-doubts for which there are no clear answers. Fundamentally, there is just a feeling of general guilt that what we had to offer was not enough to compensate for the despair of the suicide victim. A suicide note can help with guilt if the suicide victim absolves family members of blame but it can also be confusing. Maggie feels she will never get over her sense of guilt. Nancy has made a conscious effort to lay her guilt feelings to rest because she does not think it possible to be entirely responsible for the happiness of an autonomous adult.

Anger and outrage are uncomfortable emotions but very common with suicide. The feeling of being rejected, of not being important enough for the other person, can lead to rage and frustration. 'I do get angry with him,' confesses Maggie. 'Why did he have to do something so silly when he had us?' There is anger at the sheer mayhem that suicide brings in its train; anger at being left to clear up the mess; anger at being helpless; anger at being made to feel angry.

73

After the shock has worn off, survivors can feel in such despair that they feel suicidal themselves. They are often troubled with vivid and violent dreams. Wertheimer describes how some people experience suicide as an acceptable option once this path has been trodden. Nancy, on the other hand, did not feel at all angry. 'I felt desperately sad that he had to do this, but I have no anger. Neither have I ever felt ashamed.'

Families can draw together after a suicide, but they can also be torn apart. Many of Wertheimer's interviewees felt blamed for the death by someone in the family. I have known of divorced parents whose communication has improved after the suicide of a child. When something so grievous occurs, old resentments and differences seem petty and unimportant. Their own relationships have been healed through their efforts to find meaning from the mutual tragedy. But I have also seen marriages break up. If parents cannot support each other emotionally because their own grief is so intense, it can push them apart. A friend of mine felt very angry and disappointed with his in-laws after his wife took an overdose when he told her he wanted a divorce. Her parents refused to attend the funeral and never spoke to him again.

One feature of death by suicide that should not be underrated is the ripple effect it can have on friends, colleagues and professionals. When a contemporary dies in a premature or accidental death, friends feel shocked and sad. If someone's death is self-inflicted then friends feel distress and guilt. They too get swept into the 'what if I had acted differently or been a better friend?' syndrome. Youngsters especially feel traumatized by the suicide of a school or college friend. Professionals involved have feelings too. If a psychiatrist or therapist has been treating the victim for depression or mental disorder, the death can have a big impact. They carry a feeling of responsibility. It can feel as if someone has died on their watch. Professionals also might need to process their feelings with someone who understands.

So what can lighten such a burden of grief? Nancy found strength from two sources.

I had to keep going for the children. We drew very close together. At first they were terrified that something might happen to me, and I can still panic if I don't know where they are even though they are grown-up and independent. Keeping the family unit going helped to keep me going. My faith got me through too. I used to go and sit in church every day and gradually got a sense of God's bigger plan.

It helps to talk to a trusted and sympathetic friend, doctor or pastor. People bereaved by suicide often prefer to talk with others who have had a similar experience. There are a growing number of good support systems and helplines available.

It can be helpful to see a therapist who is neutral and non-judgemental, though therapy should not be regarded as mandatory. Therapists can help put feelings of guilt in proportion. A useful exercise I do with a guilt-stricken person is as follows. I ask them to draw a circle on a piece of paper and then to dissect this circle with pie-shaped segments according to the amount of influence and significance other people or events had in the life of the person who died. It soon becomes clear that we live in complex systems including work, friends and outside factors over which even our nearest and dearest have no control. It helps to remember that recovery will take a long time and will be a very up-and-down process and that grief will come flooding back at birthdays, anniversaries and unexpected times.

The emotional intensity eventually decreases. Guilt and anger dissipate. The survivors stop asking questions, having found explanations with which they can live. They feel they can move on. They may emerge feeling stronger and with changed values which they put to good use in the service of others. Many families touched by suicide have made important contributions to improving public understanding of depression. After such an event, petty things in life may be less important. Some learn to appreciate life and relation-ships more. Gradually the focus shifts from the disturbing event of the suicide to encompass a bigger picture of the person's whole life, including all the happy and wholesome times.

For suicide victims the Buddhist Master Sogyal Rinpoche suggests the practice of extra-fervent prayers.

Imagine tremendous rays of light emanating from the buddhas or divine beings, pouring down all their compassion and blessing. Imagine this light streaming down on to the dead person, totally purifying and freeing them from the confusion and pain of their death, granting them profound, lasting peace. Imagine then, with all your heart and mind, that the dead person dissolves into light and his or her consciousness, healed now and free of all suffering, soars up to merge indissolubly, and forever, with the wisdom mind of the buddhas.

I am sure that it is not necessary to be a Buddhist to benefit from these comforting and compassionate words of wisdom.

10

Ageing and dying

Retirement, which is foreseeable, can be a grief-stricken transition for men and women whose professional identity has been important. It means giving up a meaningful role, status, a sense of being productive, and outside relationships which have been central throughout adult life. We invest time and energy in work and rely on feedback from the workplace for our self-esteem. Considering what a critical transition retirement is in the natural life cycle, it is surprising how few of us are emotionally prepared for the changing dynamics it causes between partners, and between parents and children.

'We've always had a clear division of labour,' Barbara explained.

My husband went out to work where he was a senior manager and I managed the children, the home and our social lives. This worked pretty well until Geoff retired. I know he's only trying to help but he's under my feet the whole time and I feel he's invading my space. He had an infrastructure at work. Without this he seems lost. He's got no planned activity and nothing to take him out of the house unless it is doing errands for me. Meanwhile, I kept complaining how he spent so little time at home. Now I feel guilty when I go to yoga classes or meet my friends for lunch.

With grown-up children, the weight of dependence begins to shift from the young depending on the older generation, to the other way round. Like other important life transitions, planning and preparation eases the adjustment. Retirement also involves letting go mentally and emotionally of one phase of life before starting something new.

It certainly helps to have a mutually appreciative ending at work. Farewell parties, 'thank-yous' and gifts are rituals that should not be underrated. A celebration at home would be a good idea too. How about a holiday, special meal or a family celebration to mark the end of one phase and the start of a new one? It is important to plan replacement activities in advance. The majority of people retiring today are fitter, more skilled and better off financially than any previous generation. Modern medicine and increased longevity means that many of us can realistically look forward to 20 years or more of active life ahead. Retirement offers wonderful opportunities. It might mean more connection with grandchildren. It could provide the chance for learning, or doing something creative like painting. The Open University, the University of the Third Age (U3A) and courses offered by local authorities provide inexpensive opportunities for learning for which previously we had neither the time nor the opportunity. A friend of mine who was a consultant surgeon has become a carpenter in retirement. Others are making an effort to catch up with computer and Internet skills that have passed them by. It is heartening to know that Ellis Peters, the author of the Cadfael detective stories, and Mary Wesley became best-selling authors after the age of 60. There are endless opportunities for retired people to volunteer in hospitals, schools, churches, political parties or communities. If the Olympic Games are not an objective it is never too late to start a new sport. And for those who can afford it, travel opens new horizons. Rosemary Brown's *The Good non Retirement Guide* is full of information and ideas for those who want to make the most of this new phase in their lives.

I have worked with many individuals and couples around retirement and have witnessed the strain on relationships and the sadness that giving up a paid job can cause. I have also seen how with patience, humour and imagination they have adjusted and found a new and fruitful way of living. Some of the advice given for newly bereaved people is pertinent for the retirement transition. It is wise to avoid any drastic change for at least a year. There is a real temptation when feelings of loss and disorientation are strong to sell up and move from the town to the country, or even abroad. This can work out, but many people find they miss their family, neighbours, colleagues, family and community more than they could have imagined. They end up in the countryside without transport services and amenities or somewhere abroad with a lovely climate but without knowledge of the language or culture. As we move towards the final phase of life, connections with the past tend to become more important. The ageing process gets us in the end and the one certainty in life that we all have is our own death.

As our minds and bodies disintegrate, we lose our independence.

This can happen suddenly or gradually. We have to stop travelling, driving, going out in the winter. Our knees and hips give out. We can't manage stairs. We get deafer and blinder and our teeth fall out. Our minds disintegrate. If we fall on a heap of wet leaves we are likely to break our limbs. Our skin becomes as fragile as rice paper and wounds do not heal. This natural attrition of ageing creates feelings of inadequacy and insecurity. Old people are more frightened because they do not have the physical strength to defend themselves. They feel more vulnerable because they are forgetful. They worry about money. The old can get irrational and peculiar about finances. They might scrimp and save even if comfortably off; or, to the chagrin of their children, they may spend more than they can afford.

Old age is a time of increasing loneliness, as partners and friends die. In her poem 'Empty Spaces', Rosemary Dobson poignantly compares the clutter of family life with her life as a widow:

> I can cross this room
> From any direction
> To the single chair
> The single bed

More women outlive men, but losing either partner after 40 or 50 years is grievous. Old people widowed at this late stage in their lives can lose the will to live and become seriously depressed and lonely. Children may have moved away and friends are dying. In another poem, called 'Grieving', Rosemary Dobson perfectly captures the sense of desolation felt when:

> Each time a dark disorder
> A ceaseless banging of shutters

I have tried to be realistic about the losses of ageing, but we can help ourselves to cope with it positively and proactively by using some of Worden's grief tasks. First, we need to accept the reality of what is happening to us. This is easier said than done in a society that worships youth, perfection, beauty and celebrity and too easily marginalizes the elderly. We need to learn to accept our ageing bodies and minds and the physical constraints that come with them. After we have worked through this stage then we adjust better to our environment. First and foremost we need to keep mobile. Sticking to a disciplined daily routine is helpful. We need to keep busy and interested. We need to keep contact with as many people as possible. Research shows that elderly people living on their own benefit psychologically from keeping pets that give them a reason for living. Dogs and cats are there 24 hours a day, offering affection to their owners and acting as a protection against loneliness and despair. Vet Michael Gordon knows that old people can be very distressed when a pet dies, especially if it occurs on top of the death of a partner. Nevertheless, he encourages them to get another one. 'Old people worry about acquiring new animals at this late stage in their lives, but this is exactly the time they should have one. Arrangements can always be made if they become ill or no longer able to care for their animals.'

I so well remember the time when I was younger, pitying my parents because they were always attending funerals. With the insouciance of youth I used to tease my mother for wearing the same old dreary black dress which we nicknamed her 'funeral garb'. Younger still, as a child of ten, I used to dread visiting my paternal grandfather who ended his life in a nursing home in Bournemouth. He had been a missionary abroad and then a parish vicar, and I did not know him well. The home was run by nuns; looking back it was probably a decent enough place, but to me it smelt of decay and urine. I was impatient with my grandfather, who I thought was completely potty. He was always asking us to find him empty tins of precise measurements and could only talk about world disasters he had heard on the radio. I would be so curious now to know what use he made of these tins, and I realize that his obsessive anxiety about people drowning in floods in Bangladesh arose from his experience as a missionary.

The young understand very little of what it is like to be very old. They do not understand how much the old begrudge their growing dependence on the younger generation, who have to decide what to do with them. At the same time, it is difficult for the younger generation to watch a loved parent lose their faculties and turn inwards as death approaches. But, of course, we don't talk much about the fear of dying and death although it is in the back of everyone's mind. Death is still a taboo subject in our society. We avoid talking about it in any realistic details, or we wrap it in euphemisms. We describe death as passing on, passing away, falling asleep, meeting our maker or giving up the ghost. Death becomes the stuff of black humour too. We drop off the perch, pop our clogs, bite the dust or turn up our toes.

If we talked to the old about death we might risk learning how frightened they are of losing their dignity, of the possibility of pain, of losing their minds and losing control. The Buddhist teacher Sogyal Rinpoche has a profound understanding of the grief of the dying.

> Often we forget that the dying are losing their whole world: their house, their job, their relationships, their body and their mind – they're losing everything. All the losses we could possibly experience in life are joined together in one overwhelming loss when we die, so how could anyone dying not be sometimes sad, sometimes panicked, sometimes angry?

Over 600,000 people die every year in Britain. Death is something we all have to confront, yet few of us actively prepare for it. The fact that two-thirds of the population die without making a will provides some evidence for this head-in-the-sand attitude. Many couples never even discuss death or financial practicalities, perhaps in the subconscious belief that to do so would be tempting fate. We can avoid such a lot of heartache and anxiety if we grasp the nettle and plan things in advance with our nearest and dearest. If someone dies intestate (without a will), they leave their families with legal complications. There will be no executor. The surviving spouse will have to wait much longer for funds. The assets will be divided according to a rigid formula that may be far from what the deceased really wanted. Rows over wills are legendary, but rows over possessions that have not been willed can be even more bitter.

By talking and planning in advance we can keep at least some control over our death, funeral and the way we want to be remembered by those we leave behind. It gives us an opportunity to think through important matters like what we want done with our pets, or our own bodies which we might like to donate for research, or where and how we want to be buried. Living wills can also be drawn up. These do not have legal validity at the present time, but can be signed and witnessed in advance so that our wishes regarding medical treatment and intervention in the final stages of life are known to those who have to take decisions for us. Confronting the reality of death in such practical ways can bring peace of mind to the principal but also to family members who do not have to argue about someone's intentions.

Everyone longs to be able to die with dignity. If one asks what is meant by this the usual response is, 'I don't want to die alone, or be artificially kept alive on machines in hospital.' In his book *How We Die*, Professor Sherwin Nuland bemoans the fact that we have forgotten how to die in the best way possible, at peace with God. 'We live today in the era, not of the art of dying, but of the art of saving life, and the dilemmas in that art are multitudinous.' He believes that the terminally ill and the very old (with the collusion of doctors) submit to too many medical interventions. Only by being better informed about the way we die in terms of the disintegration of our physical organs can we gain more control about where and how we die. Most deaths are debilitating and undignified and he contests that we would be better served by understanding this.

> Only by a frank discussion of the very details of dying can we best deal with those aspects that frighten us the most. It is by knowing the truth and being prepared for it that we rid ourselves of that fear of the terra incognita of death that leads to self-deception and disillusions.

Professor Sherwin Nuland, *How We Die*

In his book *And When Did You Last See Your Father?* Blake Morrison spares no detail in the loving but candid description of his father's mental and physical deterioration from cancer. Some of his relatives may have found the public exposure of such an intimate subject rather difficult, but I suspect that Morrison's father, who was a doctor, would not have minded.

Coming at the subject from a more spiritual angle, Rinpoche comes to the same conclusion about openness as does Nuland. He believes that people have the right to know that they are dying. They usually know anyway. 'If the dying are not told the truth, how can they prepare themselves for death?' he asks, let alone attend to their relationships and practical issues. Hindus, Muslims and Jews take the spiritual and social needs of the dying very seriously. Family members will try to be present at the end, undertaking rituals and tasks that will help the dying person achieve a good death. Somewhere along the line, though, for the rest of us, the practice of medicine in our society with its emphasis on acute intervention and rehabilitation has lost sight of these important needs.

Thankfully there has been a reaction, and more thought and effort is being given to the art of dying. The Swiss doctor Elisabeth Kübler-Ross made valiant efforts to break down the taboos and denial around death. When she went to work in the Manhattan State Hospital in 1958 she was so shocked by the way dying patients were treated that she spent the rest of her life trying to educate people about death. She learnt about feelings and fears from the terminally ill patients themselves and was the first person to identify stages of grief in her seminal book *On Death and Dying*. When she did a study of dying patients she observed that they experienced a series of emotions. Initially, denial was common – a phase Kübler-Ross regarded as temporary and useful. Then came anger, envy and resentment when 'Why me?' was a refrain. This phase was followed by frantic attempts to postpone the inevitable, which Kübler-Ross described as bargaining. As reality impinged, deep depression set in, which was a prelude to acceptance. By acceptance she meant an abandonment of the struggle rather than happiness. In her experience, 'no matter what the stage of illness or coping mechanisms used, all our patients maintained some form of hope until the last moment'. Ruth Picardie's description of the last months of her life accords very closely to the process described above.

By forcing the American medical establishment to look at death in a more humane way, Kübler-Ross did more than anyone else to establish the notion of palliative care and dying with dignity. Dame Cicely Saunders did the same thing in Britain. The hospice movement, which she created, is continuing to grow steadily, providing places where people can die naturally without undue pain, knowing that their families are being taken care of as well. It is heartening to realize that palliative care units are being set up in general hospitals. Nursing facilities provided by local social services and Macmillan nurses are enabling more people to choose the option of dying at home if they wish.

For the first time in my life I recently witnessed what I would term as a 'good' death. A female friend of mine who was in her seventies was given chemotherapy for 18 months after being diagnosed with cancer for the second time. When it became apparent that the tumours were not shrinking, my friend and her husband took the decision that quality of life was more important than living longer. Having informed everybody that death was on its way, they lived the last few months with relish and enjoyment. Friends were able to telephone for bulletins and to drop in for visits. Near the end the drugs for her pain were overseen by a Macmillan nurse, and she died in her bed surrounded by those she loved best. It seemed entirely appropriate that her favourite dance music was played at the funeral she had helped to plan: it felt more like a celebration of her life than a dirge for her death.

I hope that a time will come when the old will feel freer to talk more openly about dying and death with their loved ones; when doctors will become better listeners and give straight answers when required; and when the dying will have more choice about where and how they want their lives to end.

Conclusion

Grief is nature's way of helping us to deal with the pain of separation and loss, which occurs on a spectrum of intensity from normal through difficult to extremely challenging. Grief is not a single state, but a changing and often lifelong process. It is a complex mixture of the physical, mental and emotional that will affect different individuals in different ways. As I have shown, we can hinder the process or help it along. We can allow ourselves to be surprised and overwhelmed by difficult challenges and transitions in our lives, or we can prepare for them better and participate in them more positively. We can isolate ourselves or we can get help from others and use the resources available to us. We can learn more about ourselves from adversity and in time use this knowledge to help others. We can deny pain or let it in. We can be reactive or proactive. What we cannot do is pretend it is not going to happen to us one day. If we love, we cannot avoid grief. We need to grieve before we can recover. We will be changed by our experience. We may well be more mature, stronger, wiser and more compassionate. We will know that we have recovered and moved on when we reinvest in hope and life again.

When I think of a metaphor to sum up all the ins and outs of grief, what comes to mind is a small sailing boat on a huge ocean. The skipper is at the tiller with a few trusty crew members on deck to lend a hand. While the boat hugs the shore, it has to avoid the currents and the odd buoy, which gives the skipper a chance to get the hang of the ropes and the weather – all good practice for what may lie ahead in the open sea. In the open sea the waves are higher and the wind more brisk and the land is out of sight, but the course is set fair and the boat is in its element. Then like a thunderbolt out of the blue sky comes the Force Eight gale. How insignificant and small the boat seems then as it is tossed and hurled this way and that by the relentless giant waves. If the skipper loses sight of his or her resources now there is a danger of being swept overboard, but if the skipper keeps faith, leans into the wind, relies on the crew and remembers what he or she has learnt, the boat will not capsize and the wind and the waves will eventually abate. The skipper will emerge, somewhat battered and bruised, and the boat will need patching, but there is much cause for rejoicing in the sheer fact of survival and the dawn of a new day.

Useful addresses

Age Concern England

Astral House
1268 London Road
London SW16 4ER
Tel: 020 8765 7200
Information line: 0800 00 99 66
Website: www.ageconcern.org.uk

Alzheimer's Society

Gordon House
10 Greencoat Place
London SW1P 1PH
Tel: 020 7306 0606
Website: www.alzheimers.org.uk

ARC (Antenatal Results and Choices)

73 Charlotte Street
London W1T 4PN
Tel: 020 7631 0280
Helpline: 020 7631 0285
Website: www.arc-uk.org

British Association for Counselling and Psychotherapy (BACP)

BACP House
35–37 Albert Street
Rugby
Warwickshire CV21 2SG
Tel: 0870 443 5252
Website: www.bacp.co.uk

British Humanist Association *(for non-religious ceremonies)*

1 Gower Street
London WC1E 6HD
Tel: 020 7079 3580
Website: www.humanism.org.uk

Buddhist Society

58 Eccleston Square
London SW1V 1PH
Tel: 020 7834 5858
Website: www.thebuddhistsociety.org

Child Bereavement Network

8 Wakley Street
London EC1V 7QE
Tel: 020 7843 6309
Website: www.ncb.org.uk/cbn/

Child Bereavement Trust

Aston House
High Street
West Wycombe
High Wycombe
Buckinghamshire HP14 3AG
Tel: 01494 446648
Website: www.childbereavement.org.uk

ChildLine

45 Folgate Street
London E1 6GL
Tel: 020 7650 3200
Helpline: 0800 876 6000
Website: www.childline.org.uk

Cinnamon Trust (helps elderly and ill care for pets)

10 Market Square
Hayle
Cornwall TR27 4HE
Tel: 01736 757900
Website: www.cinnamon.org.uk

Compassionate Friends (for bereaved parents and families)

53 North Street
Bristol BS3 IEN
Tel: 08451 203785
Helpline: 08451 232304
Website: www.compassionatefriends.org.uk

Counselling and Psychotherapy in Scotland (COSCA)

18 Viewfield Street
Stirling FK8 IUA
Tel: 01786 475140
Website: www.cosca.org.uk

Cruse Bereavement Care

Cruse House
126 Sheen Road
Richmond
Surrey TW9 1UR
Tel: 020 8939 9530
Helpline: 0870 167 1677
Website:crusebereavementcare.org.uk

Families Need Fathers

134 Curtain Road
London EC2A 3AR
Tel: 020 7613 5060
Helpline: 08707 607496 (evenings)
Website: www.fnf.org.uk

Hospice Information

Hospice House
34–44 Britannia Street
London WC1X 9JG
Tel: 0870 903 3903
Website: www.hospiceinformation.info

Jewish Bereavement Counselling Service (JBCS)

8–10 Forty Avenue
London HA9 8JW
Tel: 020 8385 1874
Website: www.jvisit.org.uk

Memorials by Artists

Snape Priory
Snape
Suffolk IP17 1SA
Tel: 01728 688934
Website: www.memorialsbyartists.co.uk

Miscarriage Association

c/o Clayton Hospital
Northgate
Wakefield
West Yorkshire WF1 3JS
Tel: 01924 200799
Website:www.miscarriageassociation.org.uk

Multiple Births Foundation

Hammersmith House Level 4
Queen Charlotte's and Chelsea Hospital
Du Cane Road
London W12 0HS
Tel: 020 8383 3519
Website: www.multiplebirths.org.uk

Nafsiyat (Intercultural Therapy Centre)

262 Holloway Road
London N7 6NE
Tel: 020 7686 8666
Website: www.nafsiyat.org.uk

National Association of Widows

3rd Floor
48 Queens Road
Coventry CV1 3EH
Tel: 0845 838 2261
Website: www.nawidows.org.uk

Natural Death Centre

6 Blackstock Mews
Blackstock Road
London N4 2BT
Tel: 0871 288 2098
Website:www.naturaldeath.org.uk

One Parent Families

255 Kentish Town Road
London NW5 2LX
Tel: 020 7428 5400
Helpline: 0800 018 5026
Website: www.oneparentfamilies.org.uk

Post-Adoption Centre

5 Torriano Mews
Torriano Avenue
London NW5 2RZ
Tel: 020 7284 0555
Website: www.postadoptioncentre.org.uk

St Christopher's Hospice

51–59 Lawrie Park Road
Sydenham
London SE26 6DZ
Tel: 020 8768 4500
Website: stchristophers.org.uk

Samaritans (offering emotional support)

The Upper Mill
Kingston Road
Ewell
Surrey KT17 2AF
Tel: 020 8394 8300
Helpline: 08457 90 90 90
For local branches and telephone numbers look in local telephone directories.
Website: www.samaritans.org

SANE (support for mental illness)

1st Floor
Cityside House
40 Adler Street
London E1 1EE
Tel: 0845 767 8000
Website: www.sane.org.uk

Stillbirth and Neonatal Death Society (SANDS)

28 Portland Place
London W1B 1LY
Tel: 020 7436 7940
Helpline: 020 7436 5881
Website:www.uk-sands.org

Support After Murder And Manslaughter (SAMM)

Cranmer House
39 Brixton Road
London SW9 6DZ
Tel: 020 7735 3838
Website: www.samm.org.uk

Survivors of Bereavement by Suicide (SOBS)

Volserve House
14–18 West Bar Green
Sheffield S1 2DA
Tel: 0114 272 5955
Helpline: 0870 241 3337
Website: www.uk-sobs.org.uk

Terrence Higgins Trust (HIV/AIDS)

52–54 Grays Inn Road
London WC1X 8JU
Tel: 020 7831 0330
Helpline: 020 724 1010 (12 noon to 10 p.m. daily)
Website: www.tht.org.uk

Winston's Wish (for advice on child bereavement)

The Clara Burgess Centre
Bayshill Road
Cheltenham GL50 3AW
Tel: 01242 515157
Helpline: 0845 20 30 40 5
Website: www.winstonswish.org.uk

Further reading

Birkin, A., *J. M. Barrie and the Lost Boys*, London, Constable, 1979.

Bowlby, J., *The Making and Breaking of Affectional Bonds*, London, Tavistock Publications, 1979.

Brown, R. (ed.), *Good non Retirement Guide*, London, Kogan Page, 2005.

Cherry-Garrard, A., *The Worst Journey in the World*, London, Pimlico, 2003.

Dobson, R., *Collected Poems*, Australia, Collins, Angus and Robertson, 1991.

Du Maurier, D., *The Rebecca Notebook*, London, Gollancz, 1981.

Emerson, S. (ed.), *In Loving Memory*, London, Little, Brown, 2004.

Fredman, G., *Death Talk*, London, Karnac Books, 1997.

Gerzina, G., *Carrington*, London, John Murray, 1989.

Gray, G., *Cardinal Manning*, London, Weidenfeld and Nicolson, 1985.

Holmes, J., *John Bowlby and Attachment Theory*, London, Routledge, 1993.

Hosseini, K., *The Kite Runner*, London, Bloomsbury, 2003.

Ironside, V., *'You'll Get Over It': The Rage of Bereavement*, London, Penguin Books, 1997.

Kübler-Ross, E., *On Death and Dying*, New York, Simon and Schuster, 1997.

Kushner, H. S., *When Bad Things Happen to Good People*, London, Pan, 1982.

Lendrum, S. and Syme, G., *Gift of Tears*, London, Routledge, 1992.

Lewis, C. S., *A Grief Observed*, London, Faber and Faber, 1961.

Morrison, B., *And When Did You Last See Your Father?* London, Granta Books, 1993.

Motion, A., *Keats*, London, Faber and Faber, 1997.

Nuland, S. B., *How We Die*, New York, Alfred A. Knopf, 1994.

Parkes, C. M. and Weiss, R. S., *Recovery from Bereavement*, New York, Basic Books, 1983.

Parkes, C. M., Laungani, P. and Young, B. (eds), *Death and Bereavement Across Cultures*, London, Routledge, 1997.

Peck, M. Scott, *Further Along the Road Less Travelled*, New York, Simon and Schuster, 1993.
Picardie, R., *Before I Say Goodbye*, London, Penguin, 1993.
Rinpoche, S., *The Tibetan Book of Living and Dying*, London, Rider, 1992.
Robinson, A., *Memoirs of an Unfit Mother*, London, Time Warner Paperback, 2002.
Schiff, H. S., *The Bereaved Parent*, London, Souvenir Press, 1977.
Sebald, W. G., *The Emigrants*, London, The Harvill Press, 1996.
Sebold, A., *Lucky*, New York, Scribner, 1999.
Stokes, J., *Then, Now and Always*, Cheltenham, A Winston's Wish Publication, 2004.
Wertheimer, A., *A Special Scar*, London, Routledge, 1991.
Worden, J. W., *Grief Counselling and Grief Therapy*, London, Tavistock Publications, 1983.

Cruse, St Christopher's Hospice, Child Bereavement Network and Winston's Wish (see Useful Addresses) produce excellent reading material for grieving children, adolescents and adults.

For children 3–7 years old

Althea, *When Uncle Bob Died*, London, Dinosaur Publications, 1982.
Alumenda, S., *Thandiwe's Spirit and the River*, Harare, Baobab Books, 1994.
Brown, L. K. and Brown, M., *When Dinosaurs Die*, London, Little, Brown, 1996.
Burningham, J., *Granpa*, London, Picture Puffins, 1984.

For 8–13 years old

Amos, J., *Separations: Divorce*, Isleworth, Cherrytree Books, 1997.
Amos, J., *Separations: Death*, Isleworth, Cherrytree Books, 2002.
Blume, J., *Tiger Eyes*, London, Piccolo, 1998.
Townsend, S., *The Secret Diary of Adrian Mole, Aged 13$\frac{3}{4}$*, London, Penguin, 2002.

FURTHER READING

For over 13s

Gibbons, A., *The Lost Boys' Appreciation Society*, London, Orion Children's Books, 2004.

Grollman, E., *Straight Talk about Death for Teenagers*, Boston, Beacon Press 1993.

Krementz, J., *How It Feels When a Parent Dies*, New York, Alfred A. Knopf, 1988.